KÖNIGS ERLÄUTERUNGEN SPEZIAL

Textanalyse und Interpretation zu

Lorraine Hansberry

A RAISIN IN THE SUN

Patrick Charles

Analyse | Interpretation in englischer Sprache

Bange Verlag

Zitierte Ausgabe:
Hansberry, Lorraine: *A Raisin in the Sun*. Stuttgart: Klett Sprachen / Vintage: New York, 2017.

Über den Autor dieser Erläuterung:
Patrick Charles wurde 1973 in Bournemouth, Südengland, geboren und studierte englische Literatur an der Universität von Newcastle. 1993 zog er nach Berlin, wo er eine Ausbildung zum Buchhändler machte und zehn Jahre lang als Buchhändler arbeitete. Seit 2004 ist er als freiberuflicher Autor von Schulbüchern und Lernhilfen und als Übersetzer im Kulturbereich tätig. Er lebt mit seiner Familie in Berlin.

1. Auflage 2019
ISBN: 978-3-8044-3140-9
PDF: 978-3-8044-5140-7, EPUB: 978-3-8044-4140-8

Titelabbildung: Sidney Poitier in der Verfilmung des Romans (1961).
© picture alliance / Mary Evans Picture Library
Druck und Weiterverarbeitung: Tiskárna Akcent, Vimperk

1. AT A GLANCE

This study guide to Lorraine Hansberry's drama *A Raisin in the Sun* is designed to provide an easy-to-use overview of the structure, context, themes and characters of the play.

Part 2 takes a brief look at **Lorraine Hansberry and her career**.

➪ p. 9
→ Hansberry was born in Chicago, Illinois in 1930. Her parents both worked and were both active in pushing back against racism and discrimination.

➪ p. 26
→ *A Raisin in the Sun* was **first performed on stage in 1959**, the first play written by an African-American woman to ever be performed on Broadway, and was an instant success.

Part 3 provides analyses and interpretations of the play.

A Raisin in the Sun – Origins and Sources:

➪ p. 35
Hansberry's play was influenced by her own experiences and her parents' activism, by the Harlem Renaissance and the poet Langston Hughes, and the reality of life for African-Americans living in a big city like Chicago in the 1950s.

Summaries:

➪ p. 44
A Raisin in the Sun is about the Younger family – "Mama" Lena, her son Walter, his wife Ruth, and their son Travis, and Lena's other child, her daughter Beneatha. They share an apartment in a poor district in Chicago. The family is about to receive a $10,000 pay-out from Mama's dead husband's life insurance, and the money causes trouble. Walter wants to invest in a liquor store with a shady friend, Willie Harris: Ruth and Mama want to invest in a nice house in a

better part of town. A representative of the white residents of the area the Younger family wishes to move to tries to buy them off, not wanting black families to move into their neighbourhood. When the cheque arrives, Mama allows Walter to look after the majority of the money to help him fight off depression and a sense of being a failure. But he loses all of the money she gives him when Willie steals it. Luckily, Mama has saved the rest and made a down payment on the house in Clybourne Park. The family gets ready to move, deciding to defy the white residents and fight for their unity and happiness.

Structure:

Raisin is a three-act play. The dramatic structure follows the classic development of build-up, climax and resolution. ⇨ p. 59

Characters:

The play is about the Younger family and a few important characters around them.

→ **"Mama" Lena Younger** is a widow. She is a strong, caring, loving figure who holds the family together. ⇨ p. 66

→ **Ruth Younger** is a weary, prematurely aged housewife. She works non-stop and is showing signs of breaking under the pressure of her work, her difficult husband, and the fact that she is pregnant. ⇨ p. 69

→ **Walter Lee Younger** is a bitter and frustrated young man in his 30s. He is intense and his sister describes him as an "elaborate neurotic". ⇨ p. 70

→ **Beneatha Younger** is Walter's sister. She is an educated, interesting woman who is determined to explore her potential and express herself. ⇨ p. 72

➩ p. 73
→ **Travis Willard Younger** is the 10-year old son of Ruth and Walter. He is a lively, charming boy.

➩ p. 74
→ **Joseph Asagai** is a sophisticated Nigerian student who is friends with Beneatha. He has a strong influence on her interest in Africa and her African heritage.

➩ p. 74
→ **George Murchison** is a wealthy, middle-class young black man who is courting Beneatha. She finds him shallow.

➩ p. 75
→ **Karl Lindner** is the representative of the white residents' association of Clybourne Park. He has been sent to the Younger family to persuade them not to buy the house there: the residents don't want black people living there.

➩ p. 75
Other characters like Bobo, Mrs. Johnson or Willie Harris.

Themes:

➩ p. 80
The major themes we will look at in this study guide are racial identity (including white-black racism and African/African-American issues): family relationships and gender equality; social issues like poverty and ghettoes; and the important theme of dreams, faith and hope.

Style and Language:

➩ p. 94
We have to deal with two distinct categories of language: the stage directions and the lines.

Interpretation:

➩ p. 99
We will look at the film in this chapter and at the continuing story of the Younger family by other authors.

2. LORRAINE HANSBERRY: LIFE & WORKS

2.1 Biography

Lorraine Hansberry (1930–1965) © picture alliance/ Everett Collection

YEAR	PLACE	EVENT	AGE
1930	Chicago, Illinois (USA)	On May 19th Lorraine was born. Her parents were Carl (a real estate broker) and Nannie (a local activist). Lorraine was the youngest of four children.	
1938	Chicago	Carl Hansberry bought a house in the Washington Park Subdivisions area on Chicago's South Side. The mostly white neighbours tried to legally force the Hansberry family out of their house. Carl Hansberry took the case all the way to the US Supreme Court, where he won the right to live there with his family (see Hansberry v. Lee, p. 36).	8
1946	Chicago	March 17: Carl Hansberry died in Mexico. He was there looking for a new home for his family. He had wanted to remove them from the pervasive racism in the USA.	15
1948	Chicago/ Wisconsin	Lorraine graduated from high school, and went on to study at the University of Wisconsin-Madison. She worked on the presidential campaign of the Progressive Party candidate Henry A. Wallace.	18
1949	Guadalajara, Mexico	Summer: Lorraine studied painting at the University of Guadalajara	19
1950–1953	New York	Lorraine moved to New York to become a writer. She moved to Harlem and became politically active: Sie worked at the *Freedom* newspaper and met Black Pan-Africanists.[1]	20–21

---

1 Lorraine's environment, work and acquaintances in New York are discussed more fully in the chapter on Contemporary Background in this study guide, see p.12.

YEAR	PLACE	EVENT	AGE
1953	Chicago New York	June 20: Lorrain marries the Jewish songwriter and activist Robert Nemiroff. Nemiroff was earning good money and Lorraine was able to focus on writing full time. **It was around this time that Lorraine began working on *A Raisin in the Sun*.**	22
1957	New York	Lorraine published two letters to the house magazine of *The Daughters of Bilitis*, a lesbian activist group. This and other circumstantial evidence has led many students of Hansberry's life to conclude that she was secretly lesbian: whatever the truth may have been, she was a vocal campaigner against homophobia and for civil rights for gays and lesbians. Around this time she also separated from her husband.	27
1959–60	New York	**March 11: *A Raisin in the Sun* is performed for the first time on Broadway in the *Ethel Barrymore Theater*. This first production later moved to the *Belasco Theater* where it continued to run until June 1960, after 530 performances.** ***New York Drama Critics' Circle* named it the best play of 1959.**	29–30
1961	USA	**The film version of *A Raisin in the Sun* is released. Lorraine also wrote the screenplay. For more about the film, see the chapter on interpretations in this study guide (p. 100).**	31
1964	New York	Lorraine divorced from her husband, but they remained close. In this year she was also diagnosed with pancreatic cancer.	34
1965	New York	January 12: Lorraine Hansberry died of cancer. She was buried on January 15 in Croton-on-Harlem, New York.	34

YEAR	PLACE	EVENT	AGE
2008	USA	**The play is adapted for American TV with the cast of the 2004 stage revival and is quite successful**. The cast includes famous rapper/producer/media celebrity Sean (Puffy) Combs.	

2.2 Contemporary Background

SUMMARY

A Raisin in the Sun was written against the background of an interesting time in US history and culture. The country was wealthy and powerful following the Second World War: industrialisation, consumerism and mass culture had become dominant forces which were reshaping the world; and capitalism and Communism were squaring off on the world stage, with America emerging as a major superpower. Within America, we are in the 1950s, on the eve of the most famous era in the history of the civil rights movement, during a critical and traumatic time for African-Americans as their leaders and activists struggled for equality. Culturally, the after-effects of the Harlem Renaissance of the 1920s/1930s are important, and socially we must look at issues of segregation, zoned housing policies in cities, poverty and equality. One further point we will look at in this chapter is the relationship between African-Americans and their African heritage and origins.

The USA after World War II

The play *A Raisin in the Sun* is set in a major industrial city in the US in the years following the Second World War. **This is the age of the superpowers**, as the war had left two monolithic powers facing each other across the globe – the forces of capitalism and democracy, led by the USA, and the Communist bloc, dominated by the Soviet Union.

Global player America

America in the 1950s was economically, politically and militarily a global player of unprecedented power. The country was rich, and its rapidly growing "soft" power – meaning culture – was unequalled, with American-bred products like rock and roll music, Hollywood cinema, Coca Cola and fast food becoming every bit as important to America's global power as the more concrete factors such as nuclear weapons, powerful industries and limitless reserves of cash.

Racial injustice and inequality

Despite the power and wealth of the United States, it remained a country with **deep social divisions**, in particular when it came to racial injustice and inequality, an original sin with which the country has never really come to terms. As the idealistic, utopian promise of the other major ideology of the late 19th into the 20th century, socialism was very appealing to many African-American intellectuals descended from those enslaved due to capitalist values, and continued, long after the end of slavery, to be economically and socially oppressed and exploited in a capitalist democracy.

White-dominated America

Capitalism, mass-produced culture, consumerism and materialism were dominant forces in American culture, but there have always been movements and groups within American society which have questioned or outright rejected this mainstream. We can see how Hansberry questions these forces too in *Raisin*, with Beneatha's rejection of George's shallowness and materialism, and the final realisation that **the family's spiritual health and happiness and union is more important than money**. The character of Joseph also poses questions about the presumed supremacy of American society and values. These issues, this discontent with the status quo of capitalist white-dominated America, has been a constant presence throughout the country's history, because this status quo produces inequality. The ongoing historical effort to correct this inequality is called the civil rights movement.

The civil rights movement

The civil rights movement is the name given to a long, long process through American history aimed at establishing **equal rights for African-Americans**. The goal was (and remains) equal rights to vote, to live and to work how and where one wishes, to essentially enjoy all of the legal and constitutional rights promised to all American citizens. This movement has been and continues to be a struggle against a white-dominated social order. The accomplishments and victories of the civil rights movement during the 1950s and 1960s are the most historically famous, with magnetic, crucial figures like **Dr Martin Luther King Jr. and Malcolm X** providing important focal points for the various social, political and geographical issues. When Hansberry wrote *Raisin*, King was still alive and Malcolm had yet to emerge: The Black Power movement and militant organisations like the Black Panther Party were products of the 1960s, coming into being as a reaction to the increasingly brutal police and state efforts to suppress the civil rights movement.

Hansberry v. Lee

The civil rights movement was not only fought by charismatic leaders or militant street-level groups. It was also a grinding, continuous legal struggle within the existing power structures, an ongoing effort to win for African-Americans the recognition, security and equality all American citizens should have. **These legal efforts are relevant to Hansberry's life** and work, as her father was involved in a landmark legal case concerning housing rights for African-Americans (see the chapter in this study guide on Origins & Sources for more on this issue, p. 36).

The Harlem Renaissance

The Harlem Renaissance is named for the largely black neighbourhood of Harlem, in the borough of Manhattan in New York City. It was also called the 'New Negro' or 'Black' Renaissance. **It refers to a period of intense cultural activity by black American artists through the 1920s and into the 1930s**. The movement was significant for the new, collective approach and for its emphasis on black Americans' African heritage.

Martin Luther King Jr and Malcolm X (1964).
© picture alliance/ Everett Collection

Cultural groups of black people

The importance of the collectivist approach was basically the idea that there is strength in numbers. Whereas earlier black writers had been individuals struggling to find a way to have their voices heard, the Harlem scene encouraged groups of people **to come together to assist one another in their creative endeavours**, supporting their writing or music or art in collaboratively organised galleries, readings, newspapers, performances, et cetera. There was huge potential for the fertile cross-pollination of ideas and techniques and energies, not just within one medium, like poetry, but across various media, as can be seen with the influence of jazz music on the poetry of Langston Hughes.

The other equally important development was the attention paid to the **African origins of African-America**. This was not an easy or an obvious topic. The cultural conditions under which black Americans had been living for centuries bred submission and self-negation: politically voiceless, treated as subhuman, abused and discriminated against well into the 20th century, the blacks of America faced enormous pressure from the dominant white culture **to reject their identity and their heritage**. An uncomfortable middle ground for what Beneatha calls "assimilationist" blacks (p. 63) is to try to conform to white middle class society. Despite knowing that a racist, predominantly white society **will never accept them as equals**, the "assimilationist" blacks reject and mock the mythical Africa of their distant past and embrace the materialist values of modern capitalist America. This is represented in *Raisin* by the figure of George Murchison, and the antidote comes in the form of Joseph Asagai.

"assimilationist" blacks

Langston Hughes (1902–1967)

The major literary figures of the Harlem Renaissance include Jean Toomer, Langston Hughes, Zora Neale Hurston and Countee Cullen (there were many, many more writers, poets, musicians and artists who belonged to the scene). Of these, **Langston Hughes had**

the most direct and obvious influence on Lorraine Hansberry and *A Raisin in the Sun*, as the title of the play is taken from a line a poem of his (for more on this see the chapter in this study guide on Origins & Sources, p. 38).

Although the Harlem Renaissance as a defined period of focussed cultural activity was over by the mid-1930s, it was a genuine renaissance – literally, rebirth – in that it inspired new vitality, focus and areas to explore for African-American culture. Its echoes were felt for decades to follow and **its themes continue to be relevant and fertile to this day**.

Society and politics

Racial segregation

The critical conflict in the plot of *A Raisin in the Sun* is the offer made by the white residents of Clybourne Park to buy back the Younger family's house. The residents' unspoken fear is that **the presence of a black family will lower the attractiveness of the neighbourhood** and therefore make their own property less valuable. This is one example of *de facto* racial segregation (as opposed to *de jure*).

De facto* and *de jure: These Latin legal terms mean, respectively, "in fact", referring to things which exist in reality, even if they are not prescribed by law, and "in law", meaning things which are prescribed and defined by law. These terms are often used when discussing the history of racism and racial inequality in the USA, because while many racist laws have been struck down or reversed, removing the *de jure* justification for racist practices, in many cases the *de facto* reality of inequality and discrimination rolls along, business as usual. A major part of the legal efforts to change things in the civil rights movement is concerned with combatting *de facto* inequality with *de jure* security. This is the case with the landmark court case in which Lorraine Hansberry's father was involved – for more on this, see the chapter in this study guide on Origins & Sources, p. 36.

Hansberry v. Lee

Segregated ethnic neighbourhoods

Chicago was, in the 1950s, at the peak of its size, power and influence. It had a population of over three and a half million inhabitants – the highest of its history, a point from which it continues to decline – and was **an industrial powerhouse**. Chicago is called the Windy City, Chi-Town, and City of the Big Shoulders[2], a line from the poem *Chicago* by Carl Sandberg, a reference to the blue-collar, hardworking industrial identity of the city. It was also, as it had been for most of its history, one of the most ethnically diverse cities in America, a true **melting pot** – but it was a city of segregated ethnic neighbourhoods.

Great Migrations

Rich white businessmen, managers, bankers and executives moved throughout the city's history into particular areas, leaving the inner city districts to the poorer immigrants (largely the Irish and the Poles) and to the African-Americans. During the Great Migrations (roughly 1910–1930 and 1940–1970), when **African-Americans left the South in the thousands to seek work and better living conditions** up in the North, big northern industrial centres like **Chicago, Detroit and New York** exploded with larger populations, more workers, bigger factories, more industry, more money, more jobs, expanding cities, more service industries, and on and on.

2 https://www.poetryfoundation.org/poetrymagazine/poems/12840/chicago

Through later stagnation and reversal of industrial growth due to increased competition from foreign manufacturers, in particular in the **metal and automobile industries**, large parts of these industrial cities declined into urban wastelands – decaying ghetto districts and dead industrial zones unable to offer anything for the people who remained there. But in the 1950s things were still looking good for Chicago as a whole. There were jobs, there was money, and there were opportunities.

Raisin in the Sun: Fear

But the Younger family in *Raisin* represent a different side of 1950s urban America. They are poor, black, and living in a ghetto. The conflict of the play is about their efforts to raise themselves out of the despair of segregated life in a squalid apartment in a poor inner-city black ghetto by moving into a house with a garden in a better (middle class) neighbourhood. The residents of this neighbourhood, Clybourne Park, are white. **They fear the intrusion of blacks into their neighbourhood**. So many things are suggested and implied by their offer to buy off the Younger family, stopping them from coming: They fear the presence of blacks, they fear crime, they fear falling property values ("there goes the neighbourhood!"), and they fear conflicts between the Youngers and aggressively anti-black elements among the white population of the area. This conflict in the play brings together a number of strands in society and politics, all of which are tainted with racial inequality and discrimination.

Pan-Africanism: African-Americans and Africa

There is no single, simple answer to the question of how African-Americans in the 1950s felt about Africa. The many different kinds of relationship were complex. This is presented in *Raisin* in the thematically and dramatically opposing characters of Joseph Asagai and George Murchison, but also in the way Beneatha, Walter Lee and Mama respond to the idea of **Africa, Africans, and African heritage**. These responses and the figures of Joseph and George will be looked at more thoroughly in the chapter in this study guide on Themes (see p. 90).

Blacks all around the world

We can look here at the underlying issue of **Pan-Africanism**, a movement which seeks to unite all people of African descent all around the world. This means the descendants of people caught in the slave trade in earlier centuries as well as migrants and any other form of diaspora from African countries.

The original idea of Pan-Africanism dates back to the 18th century, but the modern, organised form began in the early 1900s. For our purposes here concerning *A Raisin in the Sun*, it was very important for Lorraine Hansberry's development as a writer, thinker and activist when she moved to New York City, and began working for the *Freedom* newspaper. This paper was founded by Paul Robeson, one of the most important figures in the history of Pan-Africanism in the USA.

"un-American activities"

Paul Robeson (1898–1976) was a singer, actor and political activist. As a student he was also a prominent athlete. After studying at different universities in the USA, he studied Swahili (a Bantu language) in London, where he first became politically active. He worked with unemployed people and with anti-Imperialist activists as well as supporting anti-Fascist efforts in the Spanish Civil War. He was sympathetic to Communism and the Soviet Union, as were many African-American political activists of the time who saw nothing but exploitation and disappointed hopes in Western capitalism.

Due to his political beliefs, he was one of many artists, political activists and prominent citizens who were placed under surveillance by the FBI and suspected of "un-American activities". The virulently anti-Communist tone of this era is known as McCarthyism (after Senator Joe McCarthy) and covers roughly the late 1940s into the 1950s. Like many people who shared his convictions and public criticisms of American injustice and inequality, Robeson was blacklisted by major institutions, meaning he was unable to get work as a singer or an actor, as the government and its agencies put pressure on Hollywood (as well as other industries, including the publishing trade) not to give a voice to any individuals that were considered "un-American" – which applied to anyone expressing positive opinions about socialism, or criticising the racial and social injustices of contemporary America.

Against racism

Robeson published the *Freedom* newspaper for which Hansberry worked when she came to New York (see chapter 2.1). While there, she worked together with W.E.B. Du Bois (1868–1963), one of the co-founders of the NAACP (National Association for the Advancement of Coloured People). Du Bois is one of the **most important African-American civil rights activists**, thinkers and leaders in the history of the movement in the US. He was a strong and constant campaigner against racism in any forms. His most famous written works are the essay collection *The Souls of Black Folk* (1903) and *Black Reconstruction in America* (1935). Du Bois was a founding thinker in the modern Pan-African movement and his beliefs were an **important influence on Lorraine Hansberry**. While she had inherited a sense of social justice and political awareness from her parents when it came to African-American issues, it was Du Bois and the milieu she found in New York which opened her eyes to the connected, global issue of Pan-Africanism and the internationalist struggle **to end injustice and inequality**.

Culture

Broadway

Why was it such a big deal for *Raisin* to be performed on Broadway? What is Broadway, and why is it important?

Centre of commercial, popular theatre

Broadway refers to the **theatre district in Manhattan, New York City**. There are currently 41 theatres along Broadway, a street running through Manhattan and the Bronx. It has been since the early 19th century the most important centre of commercial, popular theatre outside of London. While the early years of the cinema – silent movies and early talking films – presented a challenge to the world of the stage, Broadway survived and thrived by shifting emphasis to big musical productions with big stars and a lot of show. Musicals continued to provide a majority of the successful Broadway productions, and nowadays **the Broadway scene is largely dominated by musicals**: Highlights from recent years include world-famous musical plays like *Rent* (1996), *Wicked* (2003), *Jersey Boys* (2005) and *Mamma Mia!* (2000).

1959: historical milestone

Before the rise of the pop music musicals, multiplex cinemas in every town and televisions in every home, **Broadway was one of the most important centres of popular cultural in the USA**. New plays might be toured in smaller theatres in other cities around the country – as *A Raisin in the Sun* was – but if a play was taken to Broadway and performed at a theatre there to critical and commercial success, then it had officially entered the big leagues. As we will look at in the chapter on Critical Reception later in this study guide (see p. 106), *Raisin* was both an instant success and a historical milestone when it hit Broadway.

Music

There are a few scenes in the play in which music plays an important role. Blues music coming from the radio is described as lazy, or smoky, and inspires different atmospheres in the listeners and in the scene. Asagai's Nigerian records inspire Beneatha and Walter to ecstatic, visionary dances. Riding on a wave of pride and happiness, Walter coaxes Ruth to dance with him to sultry blues music.

Black music

African-American music had been a powerful and complex force in the culture of the USA since at least the 19th century, but by the 1950s black music was at an unprecedented level of popularity, and had by this point also diversified into increasingly clear genres. These were **blues, jazz and soul music**. Over the coming years these divisions and genres would become more complex and would fuse with other streams in popular music to create entirely new genres. The first of these was rhythm and blues music (R&B), also known as "race music" by white America. **R&B** was generally faster and more energetic than soul music, driven by rhythmic, aggressive guitars or swaggering piano (in the music of blind pianist Ray Charles, for example). R&B was a primary source for what would become rock and roll music, which was a phenomenon of the late 1950s, and which by crossing the Atlantic and hybridising with British musical traditions would return to the USA as **rock music** in the form of the Rolling Stones, the Beatles, the Kinks, the Who and other legends of what was at the time called "the British Invasion". The Rolling Stones, along with British blues guitarist Eric Clapton, were famously more enthusiastic and knowledgeable about old blues music and artists than almost any of their peers in the US – Clapton in particular is largely responsible for cultivating the status of legendary pioneer bluesman Robert Johnson, who sold his soul to the Devil in return for greater skill as a guitarist. It wasn't long before home-grown white US bands like Canned Heat (formed in Los Angeles in 1965), whose members were essentially blues nerds, began to dive into the deep history of this music.

"race music"

A crucial cultural fact of these evolutions is that **R&B** was black music, and both rock and roll and early rock music were, with a few important exceptions, predominantly white. The extraordinary name of "race music" for early R&B is a perfect point to remember in the history of the evolution of what we now have as popular music.

Through the 1960s in particular, major acts like the mixed-race band *Sly and the Family Stone* and **African-American artists like Jimi Hendrix, James Brown and Miles Davis** would combine previously separate genres in creative new formats. Guitarist and singer Jimi Hendrix for example embraced white rock music, which was itself largely derived from African-American blues traditions, and *Sly and the Family Stone* cast an even wider net by incorporating multiple genres and balancing gentleness and humour with serious political and social concerns. James Brown, who had been enjoying a successful career as a soul singer, became a pioneering figure in the development of funk music, and this in turn influenced the **legendary jazz trumpeter Miles Davis**, whose career since the 1940s had been defined by restless, creative innovations, and who was constantly searching for new sounds, moods and textures for his music. Davis was intrigued by the energy (and success) of James Brown's intense, primal funk; later on in both of their careers it was Brown who looked for inspiration to Davis as the trumpeter once again reinvented himself in the early 1970s with a much more rock-influenced sound.

Jazz music

While these fusions and hybrids were on the horizon, by the late 1950s it was above all jazz music which had conquered American popular music culture. Hugely popular figures like Louis Armstrong

(1901–1971) and Duke Ellington (1899–1974) built upon the foundations of jazz music, which lay in the South, specifically in New Orleans, and created something new. Armstrong and Ellington stand out historically because they brought unprecedented levels of virtuosity to their music while still appealing to huge audiences; Armstrong with his inimitable charisma and the Duke with his elegant big band compositions. African-American female jazz singers of this era, **Billie Holiday (1915–1959), Lena Horne (1917–2010) and Ella Fitzgerald (1917–1996)** foremost among them, paved the way for pop, soul and R&B singers as we know them today.

Blues music in *Raisin*

Jazz music in this era was a powerful cultural force, constantly surging with new bursts of energy and reinventing itself as new players appeared to bring something new to the table. It was by this time less of a "forbidden fruit", which it had been through the **Prohibition era** when it was commonly associated with illegal bars and the underworld, and had become increasingly of interest to the white cultural elite. Everyone loved Louis Armstrong for his exuberant playing, gravelly voice and larger-than-life smile and personality, and everyone respected Duke Ellington for his elegance, hard work, and commitment to producing big-band music of the highest quality. On the eve of the birth of rock and roll music with the early stars and pioneers like Buddy Holly and Chuck Berry, **jazz music was absolutely the most exciting, innovative and energetic force in music**. But one thing it had not lost during the decades since its birth was a feel for the blues. Blues music, which is the music most explicitly referenced in *Raisin in the Sun*, remained at the heart of jazz, from the elegant, popular compositions of Duke Ellington to the angular and strange music of Thelonious Monk (1917–1982). The physicality and humanity of blues music, which can sway dreamily or stride and swagger, which can embrace humour and heartbreak in the same moment, is also the voice of *Raisin in the Sun*.

2.3 Notes on Other Important Works

SUMMARY

Lorraine Hansberry is remembered primarily for her stage play *A Raisin in the Sun*. But by the time she died at the age of 34, she had made a big impression and earned the respect of many significant literary and political figures.

After her death, Lorraine Hansberry's ex-husband (they divorced in 1964) **Robert Nemiroff became her literary executor**. This means that he was chosen – by Lorraine, before she died – to manage her literary work. He was responsible for looking after legal issues like maintaining the copyright of her published works, but literary executors are also often responsible for caring for the writer's legacy and reputation.

Ex-husband Robert Nemiroff

Because she died so young (aged 34), but had been very active as a writer, Hansberry left behind **a large amount of material** which had not yet been formed into finished, polished formats. The only two plays she completed and saw performed during her lifetime are listed below. **She had published articles, essays reviews and letters**. But some of her most significant work was only published or performed after her death, as Nemiroff worked to arrange what he had into a form which he believed would have done justice to Hansberry's ideas and beliefs. The autobiographical play (and later autobiography) ***To Be Young, Gifted and Black*** is the most prominent. But ***Les Blancs*** is also a very important and controversial work by a writer whose talent and potential tragically overshadowed her short life.

TITLE	YEAR	NOTES
A Raisin in the Sun	1959	A stage play. Her first published work and her greatest success.
A Raisin in the Sun (screenplay)	1961	The screenplay to the film adaptation of her play.
The Sign in Sidney Brustein's Window	1964	Her second play and the last to be staged during her lifetime.
To Be Young, Gifted and Black: Lorraine Hansberry in her own words	1969	A posthumous (after her death) collection of her writing in various forms which was adapted by her ex-husband Nemiroff into a stage play and, later, a kind of autobiography.
Les Blancs	1970	A play, put together by Nemiroff.

1961 The screenplay of *A Raisin in the Sun*

The film adaptation is examined more closely in the chapter on Interpretations later in this study guide (see p. 100). The screenplay which Hansberry wrote herself is **almost identical to the original stage version**. A few newly integrated scenes focus on Walter Lee sitting in his favourite bar, the family visiting the house they want to buy in Clybourne Park, and Mama Lena coming to find Walter Lee in the bar. Some of these scenes are mute: there is no new dialogue for them. The family's visit to the house and Mama's visit to the bar both adapt existing material and content to a new situation. The film is as a whole quite theatrical; it sticks to the limited settings of the stage, and, in particular when contrasted with modern films, has a lot of monologues and talking. Put very basically, the film communicates with language to the near-exclusion of expressive camera work or music or other cinematic tools.

Film adaption see chapter 3.7, p. 100

1964 *The Sign in Sidney Brustein's Window*

The second play Hansberry wrote, and the last to be performed during her lifetime was less successful, commercially and critically, than *Raisin*. It deals with issues related to race, but also looks at **gender equality, homosexuality, drug use and generally nonconformist lifestyles** – in a much less focussed form than *Raisin*.

Synopsis

Sidney is an intellectual living in New York who is unhappily married to struggling actress Iris. A black friend of Sidney's, Alton, is in a relationship with Iris' sister Gloria. Alton also introduces Sidney to a politician called Wally. It turns out that Wally is corrupt and Gloria is actually a prostitute; when Alton leaves her she kills herself. The tragedies and conflicts appear to bring Sidney and Iris closer to one another.

Mixed reception

The play was not a success on stage – it ran for only ten days. The critical reception was also less than enthusiastic.

1969 *To Be Young, Gifted and Black*

Robert Nemiroff created this autobiographical play *To Be Young, Gifted and Black: Lorraine Hansberry in her own words* **using Lorraine Hansberry's letters, diaries, interviews and notes**. It was very popular and critically successful when it was first staged in 1968–1969 on Broadway, and is still published and performed to this day.

The play describes Hansberry's childhood in a Chicago ghetto, her time at university, the inspiration for and writing of *A Raisin in the Sun*, and her personal life, including her illness and eventual death from cancer.

Autobiography

Nemiroff adapted the material into an autobiography of the same title (1969), which was also popular and successful. One review of a 2013 stage production writes that it is "not so much a traditional play as a collage of Lorraine Hansberry's writings, memories, and statements", and describes it as being "more literary than theatrical"[3].

1970 *Les Blancs*

This ambitious play is about **colonialism**. It was written in response to Jean Genet's play *The Blacks* (1959).

Jean Genet

Jean Genet (1910–1986) was a French writer and activist. He wrote five major novels in a burst of activity in the 1940s, including the largely autobiographical *The Thief's Journal* (1949) and *The Miracle of the Rose* (1946) and the nightmarish *Funeral Rites* (1948), written for his dead lover, and set during the Nazi occupation of France during World War 2. Throughout the 40s, 50s and 60s he also wrote several plays, including *The Blacks* (1959), to which Lorraine Hansberry was responding when she wrote *Les Blancs* (*The Whites*). In addition, he wrote essays and articles for various newspapers and magazines, conducted interviews with many literary, artistic and political figures, and became increasingly politically active throughout his life. He spent time living with the Palestinian Fedayeen and with the revolutionary Black Panther Party in the US, and an account of these experiences was published posthumously as *Prisoner of Love* in 1986.
None of the above can really prepare anyone for the unique and genuinely disturbing quality of Genet's work. His novels are **hallucinatory excursions into fantastic visions of degradation, violence and sexuality**; his plays are highly stylised,

3 https://www.backstage.com/magazine/article/young-gifted-black-belongs-page-stage-44840/

almost ritualistic explorations of power and control dynamics in various contexts. Genet was championed very early in his career by the famous **French philosopher Jean-Paul Sartre**, who wrote a huge book (in size and scope) about him in 1952, called *Saint Genet, Actor and Martyr*, which argued that Genet had created genius out of the desperation and horrors of his life.

Genet's Life

Genet's Life

His personal life was extreme by any standards: his mother was a prostitute and he grew up in adopted homes and state institutions. He was a convicted thief and prostitute who could find no environment in which he felt able to settle; a man who could find no peace, and was maybe not even looking for anything resembling peace, comfort or stability; who was imprisoned by the Nazi occupying forces and spent his later life living out of a suitcase in squalid hostels near train stations.

Homosexuality

Homosexuality

Genet's homosexuality was a key factor in his life and work, and his troublingly complex relationships to beauty, romanticism and desire are what have most fascinated readers. His political and social activism and writing grows out of his deeply personal feelings, experiences and convictions. Throughout his life he felt closest to outsiders, to the oppressed, marginalised, disenfranchised and rejected elements of society. It was this that drew him to rebellious, revolutionary groups like the Black Panthers, and vice versa.

Genet's legacy is one of the most substantial, lasting literary expressions of a true outsider and iconoclast that we have. And far from having faded over time, his reputation and influence have only grown as society continues to grapple with the dark and painful depths of human nature and behaviour he explored in his writing.

Genet's *The Blacks: A Clown Show*

Les Nègres

Genet's play was written in 1958 and first performed on stage in 1959. It was produced on Broadway in 1961 and ran for 1,408 performances. It was here that Lorraine Hansberry would have seen it: The play was much discussed at the time and shared cast members with the earlier staging of *A Raisin in the Sun*. In a play-within-a-play, a group of black actors, five of them in "whiteface" (made up to appear white), act out the sham trial and murder of a white woman.

The Blacks was successful and controversial. Contemporary reviewers "stressed the difficulty of understanding the enigmatic play [...] whereas the characters in [Genet's earlier plays] *The Maids* and *The Balcony* perform a ritual, in *The Blacks* the entire evening is a ceremony"[4].

Battle between Mailer, Baldwin and Hansberry

The play led to an intellectual battle between the white novelist, journalist and liberal activist **Norman Mailer** (1923–2007) on the one side and **Lorraine Hansberry and James Baldwin** (1924–1987), the famous African-American novelist, activist and playwright on the other (Baldwin was also openly gay

---

4 Edmund White: *Genet*. London: Chatto & Windus, p. 305.

and had been friends with Genet when they had both been living in Paris in the 1950s). Baldwin accused Mailer of viewing Blacks as "romantic black symbols"[5] and Hansberry joined Baldwin in condemning Mailer for his explosive and influential essay *The White Negro* (1957) and what they saw as his (and liberal white America's) co-opting of black struggles for their own benefit. The play's brutal but complex symbolism and themes made a strong impression on Hansberry.

Les Blancs is Hansberry's most ambitious work. It has a large cast, a complex plot, it incorporates dance and music, it covers a large period of time and it is set in Africa. It is interesting to consider this work when studying *A Raisin in the Sun* because it appears to have been the focussed of themes which were most important to Hansberry personally, and as a writer. She allegedly referred to it at her most important work, and Nemiroff describes her initial inspiration to write it as having been her "visceral" (meaning resulting from strong feelings rather than careful thought) response to having seen a production of Genet's *The Blacks*. These details and the finished product suggest that this was where Hansberry's creative attention lay at the time of her death. *Raisin* was her best-loved and most successful work, but it may have been only the first display of her full potential.

The plot of the play is too complex and lengthy to be described here: it concerns the armed resistance to a colonial power in a fictional African country called Zhembe. Characters in the play represent or are associated with colonial powers or indigenous culture,

---

5 Ibid., p. 306.

Scene from Genet's *The Blacks* (1959) © picture alliance/akg

and the presence of Christianity and its symbiotic relationship with colonialism and exploitation is also a big theme. The issue of gender equality is tackled indirectly: the only black woman in the play says nothing and has no name, being called only "the woman".

Fragments

The play as it exists was **put together by Nemiroff** from fragments and drafts Hansberry had been working on. While the initial inspiration for the play came from her response to the Genet play, the themes – **colonialism, African cultures, racism** – were already playing a big role in her life before she had even written *Raisin*. As discussed in the chapter on origins and sources in this study guide (see p. 35), Hansberry had already encountered the great W.E.B. Du Bois in New York, and she was not only the child of politically active parents, she had herself inherited their keen **sense of justice and civil rights**.

The themes of racism and power which we see in *A Raisin in the Sun* are handled in a tight environment: black-white relations and racially segregated housing in Chicago. *Les Blancs* explores these themes on a much bigger canvas – Western colonialism in Africa – and with a larger cast of characters, but racism and the abuse of power gained by historical exploitation remain the core issues.

3. ANALYSES AND INTERPRETATIONS

3.1 Origins and Sources

SUMMARY

The themes of *A Raisin in the Sun* are inspired by Hansberry's experiences and by her parents. There are many cultural references throughout the play which highlight the strong influence of other sources of inspiration (intertextuality). The main areas we will look at here are the influence of her parents and their political activism; the poet Langston Hughes and the Harlem Renaissance; and we will look at the literary and cultural references made in the play.

Premiere on Broadway (1959)

Hansberry completed work on *A Raisin in the Sun* in 1957. Philip Rose (1921–2011), a Broadway theatrical producer whom Hansberry had met at a summer camp, wanted to produce the play. He had **great difficulties securing financing for the production** (see also Robert Nemiroff's Introduction in the study edition of the play, pp. 5–14). The play was first staged in New Haven and then on 11th March 1959 *A Raisin in the Sun* premiered at the *Ethel Barrymore Theater* on Broadway. **It was the first play by an African-American woman to be produced on Broadway**. It was also the first Broadway play to be directed by a black man, Lloyd Richards.

Random House published the play in hardback in 1959. In 1961 the film adaptation was released, with a screenplay by Hansberry adapted from her own play (see also chapter 3.7 in this study guide for more on the film, p. 100).

Politically active parents

Hansberry's parents were **Carl Augustus Hansberry** and **Nannie Louise Hansberry** (née Perry). Her father was a real estate agent and her mother was active in local politics. They were both members of the Republican Party, and her father supported the NAACP (the National Association for the Advancement of Coloured People – see more on the chapter in this study guide on Contemporary Background for a brief introduction to W.E.B. Du Bois, one of the NAACP's co-founders and a big influence on Lorraine Hansberry's politics and thinking, p. 19).

Family and race

Her family was extremely important to Lorraine. As this quotation says: "Above all, there were two things which were never to be betrayed: the family and the race."[6] This certainly appears to be a true statement of Lorraine Hansberry's values, as these two issues, family and race, are strongly interlinked and dominant in *Raisin*.

Hansberry v. Lee

Beyond the biographical and personal elements, however, Lorraine Hansberry's parents are extremely relevant to *A Raisin in the Sun* because of **the landmark court case** in which they were involved[7]. Here is a brief summary of the case, and why it is important to know about this when studying *Raisin*.

Summary

The case is known as **Hansberry v. Lee, 311 US 32 (1940)**[8]. The court case was about what is called a covenant, which is a legal

---

6 https://en.wikipedia.org/wiki/Lorraine_Hansberry. This is a quotation from the essay *Lorraine Hansberry's Freedom Family* by Michael Anderson, originally published in *American Communist History* Volume 7, Number 2, 2008, available as a must-pay digital file here: https://www.tandfonline.com/doi/abs/10.1080/14743890802580131?journalCode=rach20.

7 See for example: https://en.wikipedia.org/wiki/Hansberry_v._Lee

8 https://supreme.justia.com/cases/federal/us/311/32/

term similar to the conditions in a contract: not actually a law itself, but a condition within the law which specifies and limits or defines particular actions or objects (real estate, for example). The issue here concerned **the housing in the Washington Park Subdivision of the Woodlawn neighbourhood in Chicago**. The residents were white, and they had established the racially restrictive covenant which Carl Hansberry wanted to challenge – the covenant stated that African-Americans were not allowed to buy or lease (rent) any land in the neighbourhood. The covenant had been challenged beforehand and the courts had decided it could continue. Hansberry's challenge was that wasn't represented in the earlier case.

When the US Supreme Court (the highest court in the country) had to decide on the case, they ruled that it was possible to challenge the racially restrictive covenant. Of the residents of the neighbourhood in question, 46% were against the racial restrictions, but 54% were in favour.

Pride and self-respect

The court case was important in US legal history, but it is complicated, technical and hard to follow for people who aren't familiar with the intricacies of US civil law. The important aspect for us here is **the obvious influence this court case and situation had on the story** of *A Raisin in the Sun*. The play also involves a white residents' association (represented by Karl Lindner) which is attempting to stop an African-American family from moving into their racially segregated neighbourhood. The method in the play is essentially a bribe – the white residents offer to pay the Younger family to stay away – whereas the historical precedent involving Hansberry's father was less dramatic. We can safely assume that **Lorraine Hansberry was proud of her father** for having challenged to the dominant racist society and for defeating it on the issue of whether black Americans – American citizens – can be allowed to live freely wherever they want in an allegedly free country. These core issues of pride, self-respect and civil rights are equally important themes in the play.

Clybourne Park (2010)

As an interesting footnote the real-life court case and *Raisin*, a 2010 **play by Bruce Norris called *Clybourne Park*** integrates the true history of Hansberry v. Lee with a fictional prequel / sequel hybrid to *A Raisin in the Sun*, dealing with the Younger family after they move to their new home and the continuing conflicts with the white residents. The play was very well-received, with special praise for the way it combines both a deeper, more detailed look at the **issues of racial discrimination and housing** with an imaginative exploration of the characters and scenario Hansberry had established in her original play[9].

Langston Hughes and the Harlem Renaissance

Racism and the African-American experience

The title of the play comes from a line in a poem by Langston Hughes (1902–1967). It is cited at the beginning of the book (p. 3). The poem is called ***Harlem 2*** and is part of a book-length cycle of poems with the title *Montage of a Dream Deferred*. This collection was published in 1951 and is, like all of Hughes' poetry, concerned with racism and the African-American experience. Some of Hughes' other major themes are **democracy and social equality**. He was a leading figure of the literary and artistic movement known as the **Harlem Renaissance** (see the chapter 2.2 on Contemporary Background in this study guide for more on this topic, p. 38).

9 http://chicagotheaterbeat.com/2011/09/21/review-clybourne-park-steppenwolf-theatre/

Cultural references

There are several references to literary, mythical and historical sources which evidently inspired Hansberry in writing *Raisin*. Here is a brief explanation of these references.

Intertextuality

PAGE	REFERENCE	NOTES
53	*No Ways Tired*	A religious song about persevering through difficult times and trusting that god won't abandon you. The first lines are: "I don't feel no ways tired / I've come too far from where I started from / Nobody told me that the road would be easy / I don't believe He brought me this far to leave me". The song has an obvious symbolic relevance for Ruth and Mama Younger. Later (p. 110) we hear Ruth singing the same song at the beginning of Act II, Scene 3.
57	Liberia	A country in West Africa which was founded by former slaves from America and the Caribbean in 1847. It was the first African state to claim independence and is the first and oldest African republic.
57	Tarzan	A fictional character created by Edgar Rice Burroughs (1875–1950). Tarzan is a white man from a noble British family (his real name is John Clayton, Viscount Greystoke II) who was orphaned in Africa and raised in the jungle by apes. The first Tarzan story was published in 1912. There have been dozens of Tarzan novels, hundreds of short stories, around 30 films, and uncounted comics and other adaptations. Tarzan is an extremely popular but problematic figure, and the character and stories are inherently racist, based on the assumption that a white man is automatically superior to people of all other races, especially black Africans.

PAGE	REFERENCE	NOTES
65	Alaiyo / One For Whom Bread (Food) Is Not Enough	The name Asagai gives to Beneatha is a Yoruba word, the meaning of which has strong links to a passage from the Bible: "It is written, Man shall not live by bread alone, but by every word that proceedeth out of the mouth of God." (Matthew 4:4). The specifically religious, Christian meaning of the Biblical quotation has been softened in a broader context and can be understood to mean that humans need more than physical sustenance: we need faith, art, love, community, and many other intangible things. The name is very relevant to the character of Beneatha, a curious, creative spirit who is exploring her identity.
77	Pearl Bailey	Pearl Bailey (1918–1990) was an African-American actress and singer. She was very popular and had broad mainstream success. The stage directions here presumably imply that Ruth is mockingly adopting a middle-of-the-road manner in reaction to her sister-in-law's crazy African phase.
78	Jomo Kenyatta	Jomo Kenyatta (ca. 1897–1978) – An anti-colonial activist and politician in Kenya. He was prime minister and president of the country. Interestingly, at the time *Raisin* was written, he had not yet been elected but was a more radical and less internationally recognized activist. This detail highlights Hansberry's deep involvement with Pan-Africanism and her contemporary target audience's assumed shared interest in African independence and equality.

PAGE	REFERENCE	NOTES
81	Uncle Tom	The famous main character of the novel *Uncle Tom's Cabin* (1852) by Harriet Beecher Stowe (1811–1896). Interpretations of the character of Uncle Tom are complex and diverse. The more positive interpretations see the figure as a rejection of earlier racist stereotypes, and a model of non-violent Christian resistance. More critical interpretations by major figures like James Baldwin have criticised the character's weakness and submissiveness, arguing that it is only by renouncing strength and masculinity that Tom is portrayed as an acceptable positive figure. What is meant here, though, is something slightly different. The term "Uncle Tom" has come to be – and indeed was already by the 1950s – an intentionally insulting term for anyone who is subservient, too obedient, too quick to bow to authority. This usage is historically derived not from Stowe's novel, but from later works which were influenced by it.
81	Ashanti, Songhay, Bénin	Great pre-colonial African kingdoms, the sources of much art and culture which was destroyed or ignored by European colonial powers. These cultural legacies were in the process of being rediscovered and re-evaluated by scholars as well as the activists of the Pan-African movement. The art in particular from these ancient cultures was a powerful influence on modern art and sculpture in the 20th century.
81	"The Ashanti were performing surgical operations when the English ... were still tattooing themselves with blue dragons!"	Beneatha is here referring to the practice of warriors and leaders tattooing themselves with woad, a plant-derived blue ink and dye. The Celtic tribes did this, as did many other people across Europe in the Neolithic (late stone age) and iron ages. The Romans noticed this and referred to these tattooed people as Picti (Picts), Latin for 'painted ones'.

PAGE	REFERENCE	NOTES
86	Prometheus	A figure from Greek mythology. A son of the Titan Iapetus, Prometheus is credited with saving the human race from destruction. In the reference here, as in most references to Prometheus in Western culture, the point is Prometheus' identity as a rebel who took the side of humans against the gods. The chief of the gods of the Greek myths, Zeus, was cruel, unpredictable, vain and greedy. Prometheus would come up with ingenious plans to protect mankind from Zeus' unreasonable demands for sacrifice and worship. But his greatest and most famous crime was when he stole fire from heaven to give to man. As a punishment, Zeus had the Titan bound to a rock. Every day an eagle (the symbol of Zeus) attacks the imprisoned Prometheus and eats his liver, which grows back overnight. His pain and torment is therefore eternal. The reference here made by George to Walter suggests this futile struggle against the power and will of the gods, as well as Prometheus' identity as a mythological rebel. George is also quite clearly showing off, because he knows that Walter doesn't have the first idea who or what Prometheus is.
96	"Drop the Garbo routine."	Greta Garbo (1905–1990) was a film actress of the 1920s and 1930s. She was one of the first great stars of the film industry, a global success and a recognised legend of cinema. She was widely praised for the subtlety of her acting and the expressiveness of her eyes. George's comment here to Beneatha signals that he doesn't want her to be cool, distant, evasive, subtle – her own woman. He wants the woman on his arm to be a shiny, obedient, entertaining and urbane *accessoire*. Beneatha can certainly take this intended put-down as a compliment.

PAGE	REFERENCE	NOTES
118	"Thirty pieces and not a coin less!"	The price of betrayal: the amount for which Judas Iscariot betrays Christ in the New Testament, and a price referred to at other points in the New Testament, referring to how much money is given for betraying the Lord. See the Gospel of Matthew 26:15.
123	*Mrs. Miniver*	An American drama film from 1942 about a British housewife during World War II. The reference here is presumably an affectionate joke about Mama's homely habits.
124	Scarlett O'Hara	This comment comes when the family sees the extravagant hat Travis got for his grandmother. Scarlett O'Hara is the heroine of Margaret Mitchell's epic romantic novel of the American Civil War, *Gone With the Wind* (1936 – film 1939). Scarlett is a spoiled, selfish, passionate and headstrong girl, child of a wealthy Southern family, very materialistic and very flashy.

3.2 Summaries

SUMMARY

Raisin in the Sun is a stage play, and so it has a clearly defined structure: it is divided into three acts, each of which is divided into scenes. Here are brief summaries for reference of the events and persons involved in each of the play's scenes.

The scenes are listed at the beginning of the text (p. 22), giving the general time and place and the days and approximate times during which the scenes take place.

Act I

Scene 1 (p. 23)

Small flat of the Younger family

The small flat in which the Younger family lives is described in detail, including who lives there and in which room. It is early morning on a Friday. Ruth is the first to wake up. She begins to get her family going for the day. Walter appears next. Walter and Ruth squabble as she gets breakfast ready. Their son Travis appears. Both Walter and Travis ask about a check that is supposed to arrive on Saturday. Travis and Ruth argue and the boy is sullen and frustrated. Ruth teases him to soften the mood. Travis needs 50 cents for school and Ruth says she can't give it to him because they have no money, but Walter gives Travis 50 cents, and then another 50 cents to annoy Ruth.

Travis leaves for school. Ruth and Walt argue about Walt's friends. He has plans for an investment in a liquor store and Ruth is sceptical. Walt complains about the differences between men and women and how they think and behave.

Insurance money

Beneatha wakes up. She and Walter argue about her decision to study medicine and about money. It turns out that the money everyone is talking about is insurance money that their mother Lena is expecting following the death of her husband. Walter leaves for work – but not before borrowing 50 cents from Ruth for a taxi.

Walters wants to invest in a liquor store

Mama wakes up and enters the kitchen. She fusses about everyone else in the family, annoying Ruth. They talk about the insurance money. Lena is also opposed to the idea of Walter investing in a liquor store, but for moral reasons.

Both Ruth and Lena are amused and irritated by Beneatha declaring she has started guitar lessons. Beneatha counters that she needs to express herself. She tells them that she does not plan on ever marrying George Murchison, a rich, good-looking young man, because she doesn't love him and thinks he's shallow. Lena and Ruth are baffled by her arguments.

Beneatha and Lena then argue about god (Beneatha is aggressively atheistic). Lena is furious and Beneatha sullen. After Beneatha leaves, Lena complains that she doesn't understand her children any more. Ruth tries to console her.

Ruth loses consciousness, collapsing while ironing.

Scene 2 (p. 54)

It is the next morning, Saturday: the Younger family is cleaning the apartment and listening to jazz on the radio. Ruth is not there, and both Travis and Beneatha wonder where she is. Walter gets a phone call from Willie Harris, and it sounds like he is planning to go into business with him officially as soon as the money from the insurance is confirmed.

When Travis leaves, Mama tells Beneatha that Ruth is visiting the doctor, and implies that she believes Ruth is pregnant, which is why she fainted the day before while doing the housework.

There is another telephone call, this time for Beneatha: it is from Joseph Asagai, a Nigerian boy she met on campus – she says he is an intellectual. Mama is sceptical about Africans. Beneatha's telephone conversation with him suggests that he will be coming over to visit her later.

Ruth is pregnant

Ruth returns, confirming that she is indeed pregnant. She is not happy about it. She refers to the doctor as "she", which surprises Mama. Beneatha asks where the new baby will live in the crowded apartment, and then apologises and tells Ruth it is wonderful news: but Ruth seems increasingly unhappy about the situation.

From the window, the women see Travis down in the street with other children, chasing a rat. Beneatha calls the boy back up. Ruth is visibly shaken, and Mama is concerned about her reaction. Travis returns to the apartment and is talking excitedly about the huge rat. Ruth is very upset: She grabs the boy and hugs him to stop him from talking. Mama is growing more concerned about Ruth, who is distraught and trying not to scream. Mama tries to comfort her and she collapses into tears. The doorbell rings: Joseph Asagai has arrived.

"ghetto-itis" (p. 60)

Mama leads Ruth out of the room. Her sister-in-law's powerful reaction to the rat chase has upset Beneatha, but she welcomes Asagai into the apartment. He has brought a present for Beneatha, and calls her "Alaiyo" (see p. 40 for more on the significance of this name). He notices immediately that Beneatha is quite distressed. She says that they (the Younger family) have "ghetto-itis".

Visit of Asagai

Joseph has been in Canada. He has brought her gifts: some records and colourful Nigerian robes. She is delighted He teases her about her hair, which he says is "mutilated", because she cuts it and treats it regularly to stop it from growing in its natural state. He reminds her that she had approached him at school and had said she wanted to know about Africa and her "identity".

Asagai announces his departure, and they talk briefly of gender issues and women's liberation. Mama comes into the room and is very polite to the guest, plainly uniformed about Africa but showing interest nonetheless. She immediately invites Joseph to come over for some decent home-cooked meals, slipping into her mothering role. Asagai is very moved by her invitation and concern for his wellbeing. He calls Beneatha "Alaiyo" again, and Mama asks what the name means. He explains that it is a Yoruba name meaning "One For Whom Bread – Food – Is Not Enough" (p. 65).

When he leaves, Mama mentions to Beneatha how attractive he is and makes a joke about why so many women are interested in missionary work. She leaves.

Beneatha tries on the robe and tries dancing in front of the mirror. Travis enters, unnoticed, and watches her. He asks her if she's going mad. She quickly grabs her normal clothes and gets ready to go out.

Mama grumbles about Mrs. Johnson

Mama comes back. She tells Travis to go and get more cleaning fluids from Mrs. Johnson, a neighbour. Beneatha rushes out to "become a queen of the Nile". Ruth comes out of the bedroom. It's twenty past ten in the morning. Travis returns with the cleanser he has borrowed from Mrs. Johnson.

Suddenly the mailman's bell sounds.

The postman rings the bell

This is highlighted by the stage directions as a pivotal moment in the play: it is what everyone has been waiting for, the check from the insurance company.

Travis is sent to collect the check from the mailman. He gives it to Mama. When she opens it and looks at the amount she becomes sad. The reality of the check has obviously upset her. She says that she would give it all away if it were just her and not the whole family. Ruth is exasperated by her reaction. Mama is suspicious of Ruth having referred to the doctor as "she", suspecting that Ruth didn't go to the doctor at all, but somewhere else entirely. But before she can find out more, Walter returns, very excited about the money.

Invest in a liquor store

He looks at the check and then immediately takes out the contracts for the liquor store he and Willie Harris want to invest in. Mama tells him to talk to Ruth, who is still upset. Mama refuses to invest in any liquor store.

Walter gets angry and prepares to storm out. Ruth wants to go with him, but he says he doesn't want her to. Mama forbids him to leave. Ruth is furious and leaves.

Mama asks Walter what is wrong with him, saying she knows it is more than just the money, that there is a wildness and restlessness in him, eating him up, and she can see it. She warns him that he may be driving Ruth away with his darkness, and that it is dangerous "[w]hen a man goes outside his home to look for peace" (p. 73). Walter complains that he can't get any peace here in his home. He talks about the future and about how he wants more from life. When Mama wonders why he's so obsessed with money, he says that money "is life".

Mama says that things have changed: "Once upon a time freedom used to be life. Now it's money" (p. 74). Walter argues that it's always been about money, but no one noticed until now. She disagrees. He and Beneatha represent something new. Things have changed.

Abortion

Mama then tells Walter that Ruth is pregnant. He is shocked. She goes on to say she believes that Ruth is thinking about getting an abortion, because they can't deal with another mouth to feed. Walter doesn't believe this, but then Ruth comes back in and confirms that she has already made a $5 down payment on an abortion. Mama confronts Walter with great force at this point, demanding to know what his reaction will be to hearing that his wife is about to destroy his child. He starts to speak but can't. He leaves. Mama says he is "a disgrace to [his] father's memory" (p. 75).

Act II

Scene 1 (p. 76)

Later that day in the Younger family's living room, Ruth is ironing again. She is surprised to see Beneatha coming out of her room wearing the Nigerian robes from Asagai and parading like a princess. Beneatha calls the blues music Ruth is listening to "assimilationist junk" (p. 76), puts on a record of Nigerian music, and starts doing what she calls a "welcoming dance". Ruth is bewildered but intrigued. Walter returns, apparently having been drinking, and begins mocking Beneatha's dancing and costume.

African dream

But then both he and Beneatha appear to be completely caught up in an imaginary African dream. Walter says he is a warrior and that the lion has awoken, and they both chant African phrases as he gets up on the kitchen table and thumps his chest. The mood shifts as Walter describes what he sees, and he becomes increasingly wrapped up in his vision. Beneatha is entranced by his words and the Nigerian music.

George Murchison visits the family

George Murchison comes into the flat. Ruth is embarrassed by her family and turns off the record player. Walter greets him as "black brother" (p. 79), which George dismisses. Walter gets down off the kitchen table and leaves the room.

George tells Beneatha to get ready because they are going to the theatre. She takes off her headdress and they see that she has cut her hair and left it to grow naturally. Both Ruth and George are shocked. George calls Beneatha eccentric; she replies that she's natural. She complains again about "assimilationist Negroes" (p. 81), which Ruth claims not to understand. George says she's talking about "Uncle Toms", but Beneatha explains what she means.

George and Beneatha begin to argue about Africa and their African heritage. He is dismissive, sarcastic and rude. Beneatha is furious and lists the accomplishments of the ancient African cultures. Ruth pushes Beneatha into the bedroom and closes the door on her.

Ruth sits with George and tries to compensate for the unusual behavior of Beneatha and Walter. She tries small talk but it seems cliché and the conversation is awkward.

Walter returns. He has calmed down a little. He lies about having been to New York City, obviously not wanting to seem less worldly than George. He is rude to George about his clothes and ridicules Beneatha's modern clothes as well. Ruth tries to apologise for his behaviour, which only makes him angrier.

Walter then begins asking George about his father's business dealings – the Murchison family is quite wealthy - and talking to George about his own ideas for big deals and money-making, but George is uninterested. Walter comes across as a half-drunk loser.

Dispute between Walter and George

Walter and George argue. Walter is very angry and attacks George's clothes, studies and lifestyle. George tells him he is bitter, and Walter agrees, ranting about how angry he is and how alone he feels.

Beneatha returns. She has dressed for the theatre. George compliments her on her appearance. Walter notices her hair for the first time and makes jokes about it. But George is now quite pleased with it, and Ruth also seems intrigued by the idea of natural hair. As Beneatha and George leave for the theatre, Walter calls George "Prometheus" (p. 86).

As soon as they are alone, Ruth and Walter begin to argue: She tries to talk to him but he is immediately angry and defensive. He says hurtful things ("Who even cares about you?" p. 87). Ruth stops fighting back, resigned to her painful life. She tries to comfort Walter by offering him a hot drink but he refuses.

Gradually, Walter's aggression subsides and he acknowledges the miserable state of their relationship. He wonders what happened to change their relationship to the point where they can no longer be nice to one another. He says he sometimes doesn't even know how to try.

They are growing closer, confiding in one another, and they begin to kiss when Mama comes home.

When they ask her where she has been all day and what she has been doing she is evasive, saying only that she has been taking care of some business.

Mama bought a house in a white neighbourhood

Walter pushes for a straight answer from her, but then Travis comes home. Ruth is instantly furious with him for having been away from home without telling her where he is. Mama defends him, and then says she wants Travis to be the first to hear her news. She tells him that she has used the insurance money to buy a house.

Ruth sends Travis to his room, telling him he will get a beating later. Walter is furious at the news from his mother. Ruth is delighted. Mama says they will be moving in at the beginning of the month. She describes the house, which sounds modest but nice. She then tells them that it is in Clybourne Park. Ruth and Walter both stunned: Clybourne Park is a white neighbourhood with no black families.

Ruth is torn between happiness (a real home) and despair (in a white neighbourhood). But she decides to take it positively, and seems to even be reconsidering her decision to have an abortion. She leaves to join Travis, saying she doesn't feel like beating anybody now.

Worried about the family

Left alone with Walter, Mama tries to explain her reasons, saying that she had been frightened by what had happened to the family that day. She is worried that they will fall apart: the prospect of Ruth getting an abortion has shocked her deeply. She feels that they as a family have been going backwards instead of advancing in any way.

But Walter refuses to accept her explanations. He says that she is the head of the family, it was her money, and she doesn't need his advice or permission to do anything. With the clear intention of hurting her, he tells her that she has murdered his dreams. He leaves.

Scene 2 (p. 96)

It is a few weeks later on a Friday night. The family is all packed up and ready to move. Beneatha and George walk in. He tries to kiss her but she won't let him. She wants to talk. He says no one is interested in her thoughts. He explains his very practical and mechanistic view of education. Beneatha tells him good night, and as he is leaving, Mama comes in.

Mama talks to Beneatha, who says that George is a fool. Mama sympathises, for which Beneatha is grateful. She leaves and Ruth enters.

Mrs. Johnson visits

Mrs. Johnson arrives almost immediately after Ruth. She is a neighbour. She is intrusive, overly familiar and a gossip. She relies on Mama's sense of hospitality to get plenty of pie and coffee. Mrs. Johnson warns them about attacks (including bombs) by white people against blacks who move to the wrong areas, and later gets even more specific about the potential dangers facing the Younger family when they move to the predominantly white Clybourne Park area.

Beneatha passes through the living room and is very brief with Mrs. Johnson, who takes offence and says that the girl has got too much education. She then makes rude comments about Walter being a chauffeur, and argues with Mama about whether working as a servant (or chauffeur, like Walter) is good work or not. Ruth and Mama clearly don't like her. She leaves.

The telephone rings: it is Walter's employer, Mrs. Arnold, saying that if he doesn't come in to work the next day he will be fired and replaced. Ruth replies that he has been ill but it doesn't help.

Walter at the *Green Hat*

Walter has woken up and entered the living room. Ruth asks him what has been going on, as he has apparently not been at work for three days now. He seems to be depressed: "Everything is sad" (p. 105). He says that he has been out driving: one day he went out to look at the steel mills, and then went to the *Green Hat* bar. The next day he drove out to look at the farms in the direction of Wisconsin and afterwards went to the *Green Hat*. And yesterday he was out walking, looking at the black people on Chicago's Southside and later went to the *Green Hat*.

He asks Ruth and Mama if they are now also sad and depressed. Ruth leaves.

Walter talks about how much he likes the music they play in the *Green Hat*. His mother is sad and she blames herself for his aimlessness and depression. Walter tells her that she has never done anything wrong.

Mama gives Walter money

She gives him the rest of the insurance money, saying some of it is for Beneatha's medical studies, and the rest is for him to look after. She tells him that he is now the head of the family, and should be responsible for its money (p. 107).

Mama leaves and Travis enters. He sees his father looking happy and asks him if he is drunk. Walter tells him he is never going to be drunk again. He tells Travis he wants to talk to him. He sits with Travis and asks him what he wants to do when he grows up. The boy is unsure, and says maybe become a bus driver. Walter tells him that's not big enough, he should dream bigger, and he slips into a fantasy vision of his future life as a powerful, successful executive with offices downtown. He says that he is going to make a transaction – referring to something he is going to do with the money Mama has just given him – which will change everything.

Walter's vision

His vision becomes increasingly personal and detailed as he describes to Travis their wealthy, happy life in the future, and how Travis will have the world at his feet. He becomes progressively frenzied and lifts Travis up into the air.

Scene 3 (p. 110)

Moving day

It is Saturday, one week later, and the family is moving today. Ruth, full of energy, is finishing up the final arrangements. Beneatha watches her. Beneatha helps Ruth label some boxes. Ruth talks about how much she is looking forward to having a bath.

Walter comes in with a record player, in a cheerful state of mind. He puts on a record and starts dancing with Ruth. He is teasing Beneatha about her strong feelings on race and civil rights when the doorbell rings. Beneatha answers: It is a middle-aged white man in a business suit. He asks for Lena Younger.

Karl Lindner visits the Youngers

Walter invites him in. The man is called Karl Lindner and he represents the people who live in Clybourne Park. He is very uncomfortable and takes a long time to get to the point: The people he represents don't think it's a good idea for the Younger family to move to Clybourne. He talks for a long time before finally admitting that the people who live there don't want black families moving in. They believe it is better for everyone if different races keep to themselves and don't mix.

Beneatha has been suspicious the whole time, but she and Walter are now furious. Walter throws Lindner out of the apartment.

Mama and Travis come in. The others tell Mama about the visit from Lindner: She is worried that he may have threatened them.

The family give Mama a present: new gardening tools. Travis also has a present for her, an extravagant gardening hat.

The doorbell rings again and Walter insists on opening it. It is Bobo, a frightened-looking little man. Walter is surprised that Willie is not with him. He obviously has bad news and Ruth is very nervous about his manner. Walter and Bobo had given Willie money to "spread around" in Springfield to make the process of buying a liquor store (and licence) go quicker. But Willie has vanished with all of their money. Walter is stunned by the news.

Bobo brings bad news for Walter: Willie has vanished

Bobo leaves as Mama comes in. Walter is wildly upset. Mama asks Walter if he has lost all of the money, and he tells her that he hadn't put the money for Beneatha's college studies into the bank like he had been asked to. He gave all of the money to Willie. Mama begins beating Walter in the face.

Mama is in a state of shock. She talks about how her husband, Walter and Beneatha's father, worked himself into an early grave, working and saving his entire life, and Walter has lost everything in one day. She calls to god in Heaven to give her strength.

Act III (p. 131)

An hour later, Walter is lying on his bed and Beneatha is in the living room. Both look exhausted and depressed, and there is a sense of "profound disappointment" (131). The doorbell rings: Asagai comes in when Beneatha answers.

Asagai has come over to offer to help with the packing; he likes the business of moving, the exciting preparation for a journey. For him it suggests "the flow of life" (p. 132).

Beneatha tells him that Walter has lost the money. He asks how she is: She says she feels that she is now nothing. She talks about

Medicine

what had made her want to become a doctor: the deep dream she had of being able to help people in these miraculous ways, to cure people. She says that now her dream seems childish; that the problems facing mankind are too much for medicine.

Beneatha expresses a pessimistic view of life as being dominated by crooks, thieves and idiots (p. 133), and that even independence for African countries won't change the fact that people with power will plunder and exploit. Asagai argues that that's a problem for the future; first the steps to liberate must be taken. Beneatha asks where it ends – and Asagai asks in turn why there must be an end. "To life? To living?" (p. 134)

What is life?

This conversation between Beneatha and Joseph Asagai is very important, as it contains positive and negative philosophical expressions of what life is – in particular for people concerned with progress and justice and equality.

Beneatha says there is no progress. Progress is an illusion, life is a circle, and it never goes anywhere. Asagai argues that it is not a circle – it is a straight line curving upwards into infinity. We can't see the end or even where the line is headed, he says, but we call those who don't give up "idealists" while those who can only see a circle are called "realists" (p. 134).

She says that her dreams and her future have been robbed, but Asagai argues that they were never hers, and that there can be no value in dreams and a future which are funded on the death of a man (meaning the insurance money from the death of her father).

He explains to her his vision of how he can contribute to the development of his people and his home. He then asks her to come back with him to Africa. Too much has happened to Beneatha today and she is emotionally overwhelmed. Joseph says that he will leave her in peace to think about it. He goes.

Walter comes out of the bedroom and starts hunting for something. Beneatha is furious at him, bitter and sarcastic. He finds what he was looking for – a piece of paper – and rushes out of the apartment.

Beneatha is mad at Walter

Ruth comes out of Mama's room when she hears the slamming door. She hopes that Beneatha hasn't upset Walter. Mama comes into the living room, lost and exhausted and looking like she has almost given up. But she pretends to be cheerful and wants to clean things up. She is distracted and in a world of her own, blaming herself for what has happened, saying that even as a young girl, people warned her about reaching too high and being too high-minded. Ruth insists that they can still move to the new house. She shouts that they have to get out of here. But Mama has completely resigned herself. "Sometimes you just got to know when to give up some things..." (p. 140)

Walter returns. He has been to see Mr. Lindner, the white man who had made them the offer to buy back their house (he calls him "*The Man*"). He says that he now understands that there are two kinds of people in the world – the takers and the "tooken" (p. 141). The tooken, he says, are those people who worry too much about wright and wrong. They aren't focussing on what is important in life: the taking.

He says that they will have Mr. Lindner come over and put a show on to reinforce his opinion of black people, encouraging him to give them the large amount of money he said he would. This suggestion upsets Ruth, Beneatha and Mama. Mama in particular is horrified that he would even consider taking "money that was a way of telling us we wasn't fit to walk the earth" (p. 142). Beneatha says "we are dead now" (p. 143).

Walter acts out a caricature of a black man grovelling to his white master, begging for the money. He is in great pain inside and seems close to breaking. He goes to his room.

"there is *always* something left to love"

Beneatha says that he is not a man, and no longer her brother. Mama asks her why she thinks she is better than him. Beneatha says there is nothing left there in Walter to love. But Mama says "there is *always* something left to love" (p. 145).

Travis comes in to say that the moving men are waiting downstairs. Then Mr. Lindner comes in. Mama and Ruth make Walter come back into the living room. Mama tells him to tell Mr. Lindner what he has decided. Travis, she says, should watch and learn.

Walter talks slowly, carefully, expressing how humble and simple they are, where they come from, and then he says that they have pride. That Beneatha is going to be a doctor. He will not sign away the house. They will be good neighbours. They want to move in. They don't want his money. Lindner leaves and the family bursts into action, getting ready to finally move out of their squalid ghetto apartment. Arguing and being loud and busy, they leave the apartment. Mama is the last to go. She runs back to pick up her plant.

3.3 Structure

SUMMARY

- *A Raisin in the Sun* is a stage play, and it follows the traditional organisational structure of stage plays: the whole thing is divided into acts, each of which is subdivided into scenes.
- Throughout history, the most widely used structures have been five acts (which was the norm in Western drama up until the 18th century, and which remains the standard structure for traditional Japanese Noh theatre), and three acts, which has become more usual in Western drama since the 1700s. *Raisin* has three.

Scenes

Location

In the world of the theatre, a scene is a unit of time and action which **typically takes place in one location**, in which different characters can come and go (it doesn't always have to involve only those characters who are present at the beginning of the scene). Due to the technical and physical limitations of the theatre – what can actually be done on stage – scenes in stage plays can't really involve more than one location within the world of the play, unless the scene takes place in a setting which is itself transitional in nature (for example in a train carriage, or walking along a road from A to B, in which case the changing locations will have to be suggested by a combination of text and stage effects).

Time

Similarly, a scene will treat time as it treats space: a scene will usually present **a unit of time flowing uninterrupted**, with stage time (the passage of time within the play) running parallel to real time as it is experienced by the audience, and typically, but not always, any lapses or leaps in the passage of time within the play will occur between scenes. As with the factor of space and location, however, there can be exceptions: for example, imagine a situation in which a character falls asleep on a sofa at the beginning of a scene. The stage lights are dimmed, and after half a minute or so of real time passing, another character enters the stage to wake the first person up, telling them they have been asleep for hours. This would be a very basic example of how the theatre can use text and stage effects to suggest the passage of stage time if it differs from real time.

So very basically, we can say that **the scenes in a play are defined by technical and physical factors** – one location, one unit of time.

Acts

An act is a little more difficult to define than a scene. It can be used to describe **the sections of a story** being told in whatever form. Stage plays are usually divided into acts, but you can also talk about the acts in a novel or a film, or even in musical contexts such as opera or even lengthy progressive rock songs – essentially, the idea of "acts" can be used to discuss subdivisions within any kind of narrative.

Structure

An act in a stage play is a larger unit which contains several scenes (although third acts do occasionally, as in *Raisin*, consist of only one scene). The acts of a stage play are typically organised around a rising crescendo of action, crisis or conflict, very basically, then, the first act of a play will introduce all of the elements (setting, characters, story, potential conflicts – this is called exposition), the second act will show the development of these elements around the growing intensity of the plot/conflict, and the third act will present some form of resolution to the story. This structure can be easily summarised as:

- → **Act 1 – Setup**
  Incident to begin the action
  Plot point 1 – the $10,000 cheque arrives
- → **Act 2 – Confrontation**
  Midpoint
  Plot point 2 – Walter loses the money to Willie
- → **Act 3 – Resolution**
  Climax: Lindner's offer is rejected.

The money

So how does *A Raisin in the Sun* conform to this traditional act-based structure? If we take the insurance money as being the most significant plot point, the issue on which all the other stories and themes converge, then we can see that the play does indeed obey the structural rules of three act dramas. **The money is introduced as a topic**, and then it arrives in the form of a cheque. Most of it is lost when Walter entrusts it to a thief; and in a resolution, the trouble it has caused (temptation and then loss leading to despair and crisis) is defeated when the family decides to reject the white residents' offer to buy them off.

Transitions within scenes

While the larger structure of the acts of a play tend to be more abstract and literary (determined by dramatic or thematic considerations) the more formal, technical structures of the scenes in a play are determined by the physical limitations of what is present on stage. Within scenes, there are many more fluid transitions as characters enter and exit the stage, creating new situations and constellations. This allows for an **overlapping flow of events, ideas and themes within the plot** as different characters move in and out of a fixed, unmoving situation. So to summarise, we can say that the formal structures which organise a stage play are:

→ 1 **Acts**, which are determined by abstract, literary concerns and organise the motion of the plot – this is the story.
→ 2 **Scenes**, determined by the physical, technical limitations of the stage: space (location) and units of time.
→ 3 **Transitions within scenes** – the movements of the characters: who enters, who exits, and who is present on stage.

A breakdown of transitions within a scene

We can illustrate how these transitions work within the formal structure of a scene by looking at the many shifting constellations of characters on stage in **Act I Scene 2** (pp. 54–75).

Act I Scene 2

This lengthy scene takes place in the Younger family's living room in their squalid apartment. It is a Saturday morning. So we have two firmly fixed structures: **time** (Saturday morning, with no leaps or gaps in the chronology) and **place** (one single location, the family living room). What is free to flow is the presence and constellations of **characters on stage**.

	CHARACTERS PRESENT	NOTES
1	Mama, Beneatha and Travis	The women are working to clean the flat and Travis is lounging around. Travis says he has finished his chores and asks Mama where his mother is.
2	As above, plus Walter	The telephone rings. It's Willie Harris for Walter. Mama is answering Travis evasively. Walter asks Willie if he has the contracts and says the post hasn't arrived yet. Beneatha asks Walter where Ruth has gone. He leaves. Travis asks Mama if he can go outside and wait for the postman. Travis leaves.

3.3 Structure

	CHARACTERS PRESENT	NOTES
3	Mama and Beneatha	They talk about the cockroaches and Beneatha says she wants to burn the building down. She asks Mama where Ruth has gone. Mama suggests, but does not explicitly say, that Ruth is pregnant. The phone rings again. It is Joseph Asagai, who will be coming over later. Mama is puzzled and Beneatha warns her not to ask him "ignorant questions". The two women talk briefly about Africa and religion. Ruth comes in.
4	Mama, Beneatha and Ruth	Beneatha directly asks her if she's pregnant. They talk about the pregnancy. Ruth is depressed. Travis comes back in.
5	As above, plus Travis	Travis talks about the rat in the alley. His mother is very upset by the poverty in which her son must live. Beneatha sends him out.
6	Mama, Beneatha and Ruth	Mama and Beneatha are concerned about Ruth. Asagai arrives and Mama and Ruth leave.
7	Beneatha and Joseph Asagai	[The two characters have a long and interesting conversation about many issues] – Mama comes back in.
8	Mama, Beneatha and Joseph	Beneatha introduces them to one another. Joseph leaves.
9	Mama and Beneatha	Mama and Beneatha talk, Mama goes out, Travis comes in as Beneatha is posing with the Nigerian clothes Joseph has brought her.
10	Beneatha and Travis	Travis mocks his aunt, Mama comes back in.
11	Mama, Beneatha and Travis	Beneatha gets ready to go out. Mama sends Travis to get cleaning materials from their neighbour, Mrs. Johnson. Travis leaves. Beneatha leaves. Ruth comes back in.
12	Mama and Ruth	They talk and Travis returns.
13	Mama, Ruth and Travis	The doorbell rings: it is the postman, bringing the cheque they have all been waiting for. Travis is sent out to get it.

	CHARACTERS PRESENT	NOTES
14	Mama and Ruth	They are excited. Travis returns.
15	Mama, Ruth and Travis	Travis brings his grandmother the cheque. She opens it. They examine the cheque. Travis leaves.
16	Mama and Ruth	They talk. Walter comes in.
17	Mama, Ruth and Walter	He is very excited about the money. They argue about the money. Ruth leaves the room.
18	Mama and Walter	They talk, arguing about money and Ruth's abortion. Ruth comes back in. Walter leaves.
19	Mama and Ruth	Mama shouts after Walter as he leaves.

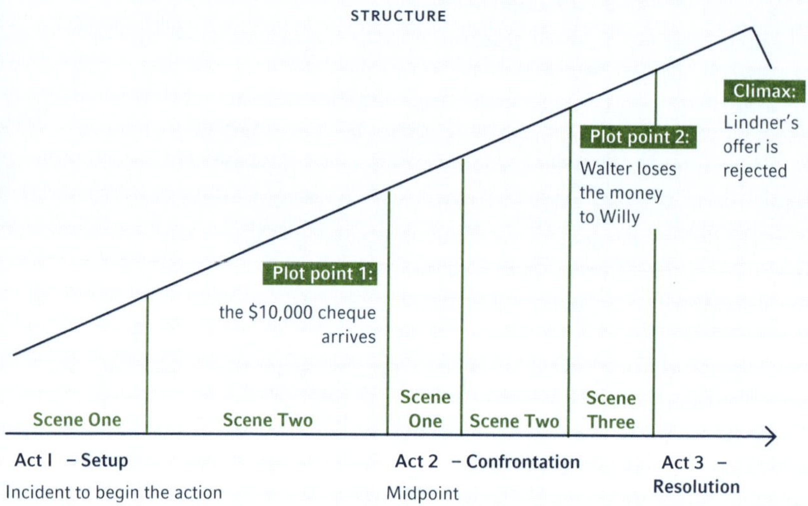

Different themes on stage

We can see that there are a total of 19 different constellations of characters within this one single scene. Characters come and go and the different groupings on stage **drive and transform the conversation, the action and the themes in different directions**. These transitions through an uninterrupted flow of time and in a single unchanging location take us from an expectant status quo as the family wait for the post to a complete breakdown of the family as the money ignites furious arguments, Ruth's plans to have an abortion further worsen the situation, and Beneatha has vanished, claiming she is a "queen of the Nile" (p. 67).

By breaking down the transitions within a scene like this, we can trace how **the themes and storylines** develop amongst the characters, as information is introduced by the author, shared among the characters, and used to drive the plot.

3.4 Characters

SUMMARY

For students, there is something very convenient and useful about the way characters are introduced in the text of a stage play – this will typically be with a brief physical description, including age, and comments or notes on the character's most important personality traits. In the case of *A Raisin in the Sun*, each character is presented in specific, concrete terms, to which we can refer while analysing the individual figures and how they develop and act through the course of the play.

The Younger family

These are the main characters of the play. There are three generations of Youngers living in the apartment (see below for a family tree) – Lena ("Mama"), her son Walter and his wife Ruth and their son Travis, and her daughter Beneatha.

"Mama" Lena (p. 39)

Mother to Walter and Beneatha (introduced and described on p. 39)

She is in her early 60s. Her maiden name (before she was married) was Eggleston (see p. 139). Mama is religious and believes that people should behave decently. She doesn't like people taking the Lord's name in vain or yelling, she doesn't approve of talking about money too early in the morning, and **she doesn't approve of making a profit from selling alcohol**. She is also shocked and offended by the idea of abortion. Family is very important to her: She respects and loves her late husband, despite his apparently difficult behaviour, for the fact that he worked so hard to provide for his family. **She does all she can to hold the Younger family together**, trying to make Walter and Ruth talk and solve their problems, and she seems to be worried that her son might leave in his anger and despair, or that Ruth might leave him because he is becoming so very hard to deal with.

The Younger apartment

The apartment the Younger family lives in belongs to Mama. She and her late husband ("Big" Walter, see below) moved into the place many years ago ("we've put enough rent into this here rat trap to pay for four houses by now"; p. 44). **While it was a nice place for a young couple, it is very crowded with five people in it now**. The idea of yet another person living there – when it becomes clear that Ruth is pregnant – proves too much, and the plan to move to a new and bigger house becomes more urgent. The apartment is a strong symbol of the decay of the Younger family and the weariness and depression which is now destroying the family (see the chapter on Themes in this study guide, p. 80).

The plot of the play centres on the insurance money ($10,000) which Mama is going to receive following the death of her husband. The Younger family all look forward to how this money – which is a lot – will change and improve their lives. Mama says that, were it not for her family, she would donate the money to charity. As it is, she wants to use part of the money to pay for Beneatha's education, and the rest of it to pay for a house in a different part of town. The conflict in the play arises from her son Walter's wish to use the money to invest in a liquor store with his friend Willie Harris. **Mama objects to this on moral grounds**; Ruth objects because she doesn't trust Willie.

Mama wants to help the depressed Walter

When the money arrives, Mama sees how humiliated and depressed Walter is by his sense of failure and impotence, and she lets him manage the money **to give him a sense of self-worth**. Walter loses all the money she gave him when Willie steals it. Mama had kept enough, however, to make the down payment for the house in Clybourne Park.

Mama is probably **the most powerful character in the play**, in the sense that her actions have the greatest influence. She holds the family together on a larger scale, whereas Ruth is responsible for the daily business (getting Travis ready for school, doing the laundry, et cetera). She supports Ruth when she despairs of Walter, and allows Beneatha the space she needs to discover herself. She sees the pain in her son and does what she can to support him, while guiding him with rules and sometimes biblically founded **laws for morally correct behaviour** (see in particular her righteous fury concerning the abortion, p. 75).

Strong character

She is also, quite clearly, the character for whom Lorraine Hansberry has the most affection and respect. She is described (p. 39) as being **beautiful, strong and noble**. It is her strength and nobility which holds the Younger family together and which saves it in the end. Her decision to buy the house in Clybourne Park and get the family out of the ghetto and poverty in which they have been living – and which is destroying them – is a bold step, but one which, as we see at the end of the play, allows the family to rediscover its unity and pride. She allows them to see the future and to imagine a better time and place for all of them. She is guided by love, common-sense, and principles.

Symbol of life

Mama's houseplant

This plant is mentioned every now and again throughout the play. It is a quiet symbol of Mama's power to nurture and protect the things she loves. The plant is first introduced on p. 39 – it is the first thing Mama does when she wakes up: "*She crosses through the room, goes to the window, opens it, and brings in a feeble little plant growing doggedly in a small pot on the windowsill. She feels the dirt and puts it back out.*"

Look at the adjectives used: the plant is "*feeble*" but it is "*dogged*". It is weak but has not given up. The symbolism is very clear here. The plant is life: responsibility; love; something to care for. However weakened it is, Mama looks after it and makes sure it's still hanging on.
The symbolic significance of this quiet little plant is reinforced by the very last line of the play. The lights have already gone down, and the curtain is about to fall on the performance: Mama has been the last figure to exit the stage. "*The door opens and she comes back in, grabs her plant, and goes out for the last time.*" (p. 151) The plant, like the Younger family, has survived thanks to Mama's care, nurturing and love.

Ruth (p. 24)

Walter's wife and Travis' mother

About 30 years old, Ruth is Walter's wife and Travis' mother. Ruth is introduced as the character who does the daily business of the family and keeps the household running. She works non-stop, from when she wakes up until she passes out unconscious while ironing. She is the person responsible for getting Travis and Walter going in the morning; for keeping a sensible attitude to money; for making sure that people have enough to eat; for running the household. But even the burdens of her work and the family's poverty and cramped conditions can't suppress her **fundamental warmth**, as we can see when she defuses arguments with her son and husband by gently teasing them.

Practical woman

Ruth is introduced to us as a practical woman. **She works hard in every way** – not only in keeping the family and household running, but in keeping the peace and smoothing over small conflicts within the family. She is practical rather than sentimental, and she is presented from the first as being evidently very, **very different from the more artistically-inclined Beneatha** (look at how she reacts to Beneatha's attitude towards subjects like learning, self-expression and boyfriends).

But Ruth is also pregnant, exhausted, and battling despair. Her husband Walter is a difficult, demanding man, and while Travis is a sweet kid, he is also a 10-year old boy who requires constant supervision. Her sister-in-law Beneatha is a clever, interesting woman, but she is concerned with her own life. When Ruth comes close to breaking **it is Mama who picks her up and supports her**.

No time for dreams

Her life is hard because of both the non-stop work she has to do in conditions of poverty and hardship, and the emotional burden of her intense and permanently angry husband. These pressures have aged her prematurely: When she is introduced we are told that "*she was a pretty girl*" (p. 24) but that she has been marked by the weight of **disappointments in a life which was not what she had expected**. Walter deals with his dreams by sinking into bitterness and anger and hanging out in bars with his friends, and Beneatha is a more carefree figure, supported by her loving family, enjoying her explorations of life and what it has to offer her. For Ruth there is only the grinding, never-ending work of running a household. Ruth has no time for dreams, nor energy for anything but work.

Walter Lee (p. 25)

Ruth's husband, Travis' father, brother to Beneatha and son to Lena

Walter is in his mid-30s. He is "a lean, intense young man [...] always in his voice there is a quality of indictment" (p. 25). His sister Beneatha describes him as an "elaborate neurotic" (p. 49). Walter is frustrated by circumstances at the beginning of the play: He is keenly aware of the injustice of being a black man in a racist society, and he feels that he is not receiving the support he deserves and needs from his wife.

Walter has a tendency to dream and fantasize. He becomes completely wrapped up in his fantasies of a mythical African alter ego, "Flaming Spear" (pp. 77–80), and he becomes equally entranced by his vision of his own future as a successful executive working in offices downtown (see pp. 108–109, for example). He talks early in the play about dreams, and about how the stifling of his dreams is killing him as a man.

Dreams

The theme of dreams is strong throughout the play, and Walter is one of its most important vehicles. **He is bitter, frustrated and angry because he feels unable to be a man**. Poverty and circumstance, depression and frustration have taken away his energy, his hope, and his opportunities. He drinks to escape his reality, losing himself in fantasies of masculine dominance and superiority, whether as a mighty African hunter or as a powerful suit-wearing executive in the city. He feels that the women around him, in particular his wife, are not supporting him in his quest to pursue his dreams. This conflict within the family is one of the most painful parts of the story, because trapped as he is in his own suffering, Walter inflicts a great deal of pain on Ruth, who is doing all she can without pause to support her family.

Self-pity

Another aspect of Walter's character which we shouldn't overlook is his self-pity. He feels that he is getting a rough deal from everyone and everything, and he likes to blame black women (in general, and his wife in particular) for failing to support him. His sense of bitterness, frustration, anger and neglect manifests in different ways throughout the play, but a constant undercurrent is self-pity. **He drinks because he feels sorry for himself**. To look at a specific example: When his wife dismisses Willie Harris as a "good-for-nothing loudmouth" Walter responds, "Anybody who talks to me has got to be a good-for-nothing loudmouth, ain't he?" (p. 32). That is of course absolutely not what Ruth had said, but Walter is once again feeling sorry for himself, and perceiving everything as an attack on him. He attempts to blame his failures in life on other people's interference and efforts to limit him, and doesn't seem to look within himself for the answers. He is in many ways his own worst enemy.

Irresponsibility

Walter Lee **works as a chauffeur, a job which he hates** (see p. 73), and he risks his job and income by missing work. He has a very irresponsible attitude to money, which is important to both his character **(an egotist and a dreamer)** and to the plot (his careless, reckless behaviour when Mama gives him control of the majority of the insurance money). Walter Lee's irresponsibility when it comes to money – from giving his son 50 cents at the beginning which he then has to borrow back from his wife, to losing nearly $10,000 to a conman – is an important element of his nature and the story.

Beneatha "Bennie" (p. 35)

Walter's sister

Beneatha, about 20 years old and more educated than the rest of the family, wants to study to become a doctor. She also once wanted to learn horseback riding, photography, and now she wants to learn to play guitar (p. 47). Beneatha doesn't seem to be able to concentrate on one thing, her family feels. She appears to have made herself comfortable living with her family. "I experiment with different forms of expression" (p. 48) – she has artistic impulses and instincts, but those around her worry that **she lacks focus and discipline**.

➪ See Sample Exam Questions, p. 117

Complicated figure: "a new woman"

Beneatha is a complicated figure, more subtle and more cultured than the others in the play. She has enormous potential, and she knows this, too. Where her brother Walter has dreams, Beneatha has plans. She is situated thematically and symbolically between the "assimilationist", middle-class George Murchison and the "intellectual" Nigerian student Joseph Asagai (see below for more on this). But she is also **an intelligent and strong-willed young woman** who refuses to define herself by the men around her. She is compassionate and loving, despite her self-focussed, exploratory personality.

Travis Willard (p. 25)

Ruth and Walter's son

Travis is described as being 10 or 11 years old. He adapts to his environment: He is happy chasing rats in the alley because it's the world he knows. While the Younger family is poor, they are a loving, supportive group, and **Travis is much loved** by his mother and grandmother particularly.

Travis does not play a large role in the action of the play. He is more important as a measure of the family's emotional health. He can bring warmth out of Ruth, even when she is exhausted and upset by her husband (see pp. 29–30). The scene with the rats highlights the poor living conditions of the family because Travis, as the youngest member, represents the future, and **they see their future chasing rats in a ghetto back alley** (see p. 59).

Life and future

Travis is a young boy and lacks the power of Mama or Ruth. He is also too young to be burdened with his father's frustrated dreams or organising his own potential, like his aunt Beneatha. Travis represents the future and the unquestioning, unambiguous fact of love in the world of *A Raisin in the Sun*. He is young enough to still be able to adapt to his environment, so it is of paramount importance that he be removed from the crushing, desperate world of the ghetto.

The other characters

Joseph Asagai (p. 60)

A Nigerian student who is courting Beneatha

Joseph calls Beneatha on the Saturday the cheque is due to arrive (p. 56). Beneatha describes him as an intellectual, and met him on the college campus. He turns up later that day to visit her (see Act I Scene 2, from p. 60). He is described as a "*dramatic-looking young man*". Mama thinks he's very attractive.

Joseph refers to Beneatha as "Alaiyo", which is a name in the Yoruba language meaning "She For Whom Bread Is Not Enough" (see p. 65). He also gives her his sister's traditional Nigerian clothes, a dress and headdress, as well as some records of Nigerian music. These clothes have an alternately comic and powerful effect on both Beneatha and Walter. Beneatha's efforts to take on a Nigerian identity by literally putting on Nigerian clothes is symbolically and thematically important (see more on race and identity in the chapter on Themes later in this study guide, p. 90). But aside from the satire and comedy of this moment, there is **the vision of an African identity** which seizes control of both Beneatha and Walter when he comes home, drunk, and sees her and hears the African music. Walter becomes "Flaming Spear", the mighty African hunter, and Beneatha becomes a tribal woman caught up in a trance-like ritual dance (p. 77–80).

Pride in being black

Joseph provides an alternative perspective on the themes in the play, including the ideas of dignity, pride in being black, **African heritage and culture**, and concepts of liberation. He also serves as a polar opposite to George Murchison, Beneatha's other suitor.

George Murchison (p. 79)

"That's what being eccentric means – being natural." (p. 80)

A young man Beneatha is seeing, rich and good-looking but shallow, according to Beneatha. When we finally meet him, at the beginning of Act II, he is dressed in urbane and fashionable clothes (see description p. 83).

He is contemptuous of Beneatha and Walter's spontaneous celebration of their African heritage. **He argues with Beneatha about her fascination with ancient African cultures**: He has nothing but contempt for what she claims to value. He appears as a pedantic know-it-all, when he answers Ruth for example: "It's an eight-thirty curtain. That's just Chicago, though. In New York, standard curtain time is eight-forty." (p. 82)

A polar opposite to Joseph Asagai

George is presented in the play as being a polar opposite to Joseph Asagai. The two men, both trying to get closer to Beneatha, represent conflicting influences and worlds (see below for an examination of this particular triangular constellation of characters). George is "assimilationist" – **he seems to be trying to deny his blackness and his African-ness**. His rejection of the "natural" (see quotation above) should already mark him for us as a character who is not entirely positive, because what he is rejecting is Beneatha's wish to grow her hair naturally and celebrate her specifically black beauty.

Karl Lindner (p. 113)

Only white person in the play

A middle-aged cultivated white man who represents the people who live in Clybourne Park. He brings the Youngers a message that they will not be welcome in the white area, and an offer to buy their house from them. Lindner is a fussy character, unwilling to speak plainly and be honest about **the racism behind the residents' offer** to the Younger family.

Mrs. Johnson (p. 98)

Her family shares the bathroom with the Youngers

A "*squeaky wide-eyed lady of no particular age*", Mrs. Johnson is a neighbour in the house where the Younger family live. Mama borrows cleaning stuff from her, and dismisses Mrs. Johnson as being **tight-fisted and ungenerous**, despite having borrowed so much baking powder from Mama over the years.

She is "a woman who decided long ago to be enthusiastic about EVERYTHING in life" (p. 99). She comes by to visit when the Youngers are packed up and ready to move. She is presented to us as being **a fake and shallow person**, and is treated as such by Ruth and Mama: She seems to be a gossip, someone who likes to harvest details from her neighbours' lives. She is an ignorant, crude woman, and Beneatha comments that she (meaning black people like her, ignorant and crude) is one of the two great problems black people must overcome (the other being the Ku Klux Klan).

Caricature of the curious neighbour

Mrs. Johnson is, in the context of the plot, merely an irritation. In the larger thematic context of the play, **she represents a backward, ignorant and toxic type of character** displaying ghetto-bred, mean-spirited and petty behaviour. She serves as an example of why it is so important for the Younger family to seize the initiative, to act on their pride and their dreams for a better future, and to get out of the squalor of their environment and find somewhere healthier.

Bobo (p. 125)

Not bright

A small and wretched figure who had planned on going in on the liquor store deal with Walter and Willie. He brings Walter the news that Willie has stolen all of both their money and vanished.

Characters who are mentioned but do not appear on stage:
These figures are talked about but are either dead or not present in the action of the play.

"Big" Walter Younger (deceased)

Lena's husband, Beneatha and Walter's father

The $10,000 insurance money comes from his death. The flat the Younger family lives in was the first place he and Lena lived in when they married.

Big Walter is mentioned a couple of times as **an example of what a man should be**. Despite having been an apparently difficult man, given to drinking, womanising and, it is implied, violence (see p. 45 for Mama's recollections of her husband's character), Mama speaks fondly and proudly of him as a man who **worked hard and lived well**. He remains a shadowy figure looming over Walter Lee, an example of manliness from another age, a role model he feels unable to live up to.

Willie (Willy) Harris

"a good-for-nothing loud-mouth" (p. 32)

A friend of Walter's who has a plan to invest in a liquor store. He calls Walter on the Saturday (p. 54). He is trying to persuade Walter (and Bobo) to join him in investing in a liquor store, a plan which both Lena and Ruth Younger are opposed to. Willie is pressuring Walter into making the investment, and when Walter finally gets his hands on the money, Willie runs off with all of it (including Bobo's investment – see pp. 127–128). As Ruth had correctly intuited, **Willie Harris is a shady character**, an untrustworthy thief.

Note: Willie is written as both Will*y* (see p. 32) and Will*ie* (see p. 54) in the play.

Constellation of the characters

Because the characters in *Raisin* are all (with a few exceptions) **members of the same family**, it is easy to organise them and identify their relationships when we want to begin analysing them individually and as units within the bigger picture.

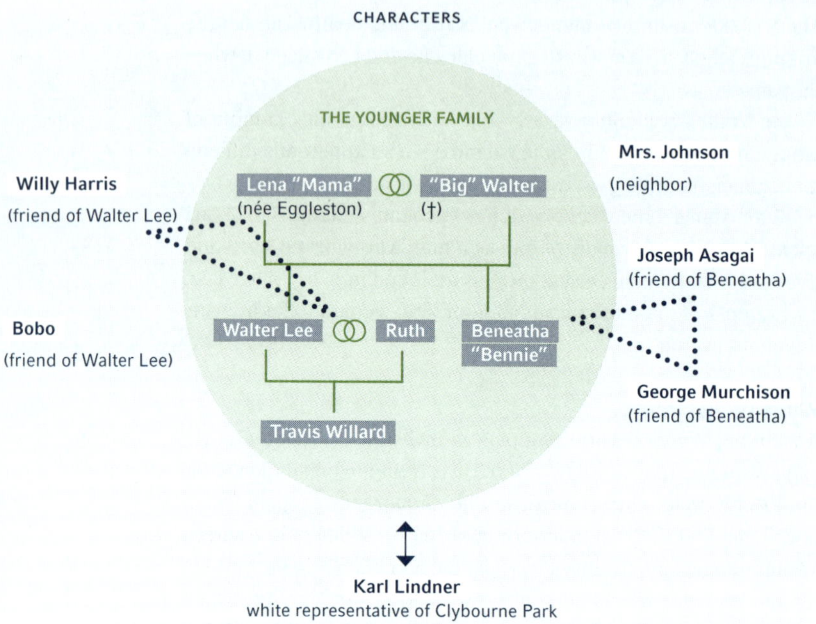

A simple family tree clearly and precisely lays out how the characters fit together.

The family tree structure is a wonderfully simple format which also allows us to view the characters through time: family trees are generational, they take us from the past (at the top of the page) to the present day (at the bottom of the page). This arrangement of the characters helps us when looking at themes related to **generational conflicts and developments and changes in society**. With

Mama at the top of the tree, representing the "old world", we have a perspective on three generations of African-Americans in Chicago.

Triangles

There are triangular constellations of characters in the play which highlight some of the most important themes. These triangles show main characters being caught between polar opposites, symbolising the thematic conflicts the play explores. Here we can **look at two of the most important triangular constellations** of characters in the play.

Important themes

Beneatha is a character who symbolises many of the larger themes of **identity, African origins and the place of black people in white-dominated US society**. These issues and conflicts are perfectly embodied by the triangle of:

→ **George Murchison**
→ **Beneatha**
→ **Joseph Asagai**.

Walter is another character caught in a triangle which symbolises and explores themes in the play. He is torn between the influences of Willie Harris, who eventually steals all of his money, and the more cautious and sensible women in his family, his wife Ruth and his mother. Walter struggles in this context with his burning need to be a man, to make decisions, to make bold moves to ensure his family's future prosperity. He is motivated by **poverty, frustration, desperation and bitterness**. The women are more cautious and for different reasons distrust the plan to invest in a liquor store. The moral dangers inherent in the enterprise finally come true when the plan leads to Walter losing all of the family's money to a thief.

How a man should be

3.5 Notes on themes

SUMMARY

The play is about the efforts of an African-American family in Chicago in the 1950s to get out of poverty and the ghetto. The major themes are racial identity, family relationships (including questions of gender equality), social issues like poverty, and the importance of dreams, faith and hope. Other issues like money and the diverse relationships African-Americans have to their African origins are also important.

Poverty and money

"Once upon a time freedom used to be life. Now it's money." (p. 74)

TEXT	REFERENCE	NOTES
[opening stage directions]	(see pp. 23–24)	The setting and scenario of the play tell us how the Younger family are living. Look at the words used to describe the apartment in the stage directions at the beginning: tired, weariness, depressing uniformity, and so on.
[breakfast conversations between Ruth, Travis and Walter]	(pp. 28–32)	Money is an issue from the very beginning, with Travis asking for 50 cents, his mother telling him he can't have it because they haven't enough money, and then Walter Lee giving the boy the coins and having to ask his wife to borrow some because now he has none. The comedy in this scene highlights a difficult fact of life for the Younger family, a very real and practical problem.

TEXT	REFERENCE	NOTES
"Listen, man, I got some plans that could turn this city upside down." (p. 84)	(pp. 83–85)	Walter tries to interest George in his ideas. But George, who comes from a wealthy family, sees right through Walter's hopeless and ridiculous dreams, and sees that Walter is just trying to scavenge more money for some doomed investment. George's dismissive response to Walter is insulting but rational. Walter has been drinking and speaks with the desperation of poverty and need.
"You don't understand yet, son, but your daddy's gonna make a transaction... [...]." (p. 108)	(pp. 108–109)	Walter's frustration and anger at his place in life, and his self-pity at his own inability to accomplish anything or become something greater than what he is, is inextricably tied up with money. He is poor and he feels poor. He fantasises about wealth and the kind of status only money can bring in a materialist, capitalist society. His fantasies are (with the exception of his drunken reaction to Asagai's Nigerian music) about wealth.
"Oh Lord, they're chasing a rat!" (p. 58)	(pp. 58–59)	The scene where Travis is chasing a rat down in the alley by the apartment building is an important moment in the play's depiction of the pressures on the Younger family. This is a very visceral illustration of poverty: a bright and well-loved child of 10 has nothing better to do with his time at the weekend than hunt vermin in an alleyway. This is a pretty blunt glimpse into ghetto life, in all its ugliness, poverty and hopelessness.

TEXT	REFERENCE	NOTES
Mama: "Son – how come you talk so much 'bout money?" Walter: (*With immense passion*) "Because it is life, Mama!" (p. 74)	(p. 74)	The conversation between Mama and Walter about the nature of money, and the assertion that money is life, is another important passage for the topic of poverty and money. This attitude feels wrong. The brutal reduction to money of everything that life could be is the tragedy of poverty, because what it really means, as we see in the play, is the denial of any kind of opportunity or chance to improve life. There is no nobility in poverty or ghetto life: it's a brutal and oppressive state to live in, crushing spirits (Walter Lee) and prematurely ageing the hard-working (Ruth). Lena's solid foundation of faith and strength helps her, and Beneatha's broader horizons – her confidence that there is more to life than this – are the positive sources of energy within the play, an energy which refuses to be limited and held down by poverty. As a note here on Walter's character, the stage directions ("*With immense passion*") are very significant. Walter's fixation on money above all else – including his wife's well-being and happiness – is seen here at its most explicit in this scene.

Family relationships and gender issues

Family – stay together!

The family is extremely important in *Raisin*. These people look out for one another, and struggle to stay together. Across generations, from Lena to Travis, **they are bound by love and the strength of their family ties**. The main point of the play, alongside the issue of racial discrimination, is the strength of family and the resilience of these bonds under enormous pressures from within (Walter's bitter anger and Ruth's exhaustion) and without (poverty and environment).

Gender roles are also an issue for Lorraine Hansberry, more explicitly so in her later work and writings than in *Raisin*, but the questions of male and female relationships and gender inequality are also present here.

TEXT	REFERENCE	NOTES
(1) Walter: That is what is wrong with the colored woman in this world ... Don't understand about building their men up and making 'em feel like they somebody." (p. 34) (2) Ruth to Travis: "I wouldn't kiss that woman good-bye for nothing in this world this morning!" (p. 30) (3) [After Beneatha talks about how god doesn't exist] (Mama *absorbs this speech, studies her daughter and rises slowly and crosses to* Beneatha *and saps her powerfully across the face. After, there is only silence and the daughter drops her eyes from her mother's face, and Mama is very*	(1) pp. 33–35 (2) p. 30 (3) p. 51	Family dynamics are relevant in the play because of the demands the characters place on one another. Walter Lee demands support from his wife (1): Ruth demands affection from her son (2); Lena demands obedience and decency from her children (3). These three scenes tell us a lot about each of the characters involved. Walter is a passive-aggressive, self-pitying man who deals with his own frustration, inadequacy and failure by attacking those closest to him, most often his wife. Ruth is physically exhausted and emotionally battered but still summons the strength to tease and banter with her son, cajoling him into giving her a kiss good-bye. Being a good kid who knows how much his mother loves him and how much he loves her, Travis drops his sulky act and hugs her.

TEXT	REFERENCE	NOTES
tall before her) "Now – you say after me, in my mother's house there is still God." (p. 51)		The scene with Beneatha's blasphemy shows Mama at her most formidable. She not only strikes her daughter, she also forces Beneatha to submit to her.
[Act I scene 1]	(pp. 23–53)	We can look at the emotional demands Walter Lee places on Ruth in contrast with how she works herself to exhaustion to look after the family. With seemingly no concern for her feelings or state of mind, Walter heaps abuse on her and punishes her for his own feelings of inadequacy, blaming her (and black women in general) for his frustration and failure. These scenes between the two are interesting when considering the wife-husband dynamics within the family, as well as the general male-female relationship and the more specific issue of African-American gender roles in US society in this time (the 1950s).
Asagai: "For a woman it should be enough." Beneatha: "I know – because that's what it says in all the novels that men write." [...] Asagai: "It's how you can be sure that the world's most liberated women are not liberated at all. You all talk about it too much!" (pp. 63–64)	(pp. 60–66)	The other important scene concerning this topic is the conversation between Beneatha and Joseph Asagai. This contains more global thoughts about the liberation of women in male-dominated societies, as Asagai compares the status of women in his home country of Nigeria with that of the supposedly more liberated women of the USA. This conversation is very important because it touches on many of the larger topics (beyond the issues facing a poor black family in Chicago in the 1950s) which interested Lorraine Hansberry, including global gender issues and Pan-Africanism.

TEXT	REFERENCE	NOTES
[Walter becomes Flaming Spear, mighty hunter and warrior]	(pp. 77–79)	Both Beneatha and Walter are here caught in a kind of trance, which the stage directions suggest is more than just drunken fooling around ("*It is the inner* Walter *speaking: the Southside chauffeur has assumed an unexpected majesty*"). This is the one occasion in the play when we see Walter shake off his frustrated bitterness as well as his foolish obsession with money and Willie Harris' plans for the liquor store. Under the influence of alcohol and Beneatha's Nigerian phase, with her music, clothes and dancing, Walter somehow touches a traditional, tribal masculine strength within him, an echo or vision of his African heritage. For those around the two of them, their performance is absurd and ridiculous (Ruth and George both have little patience with it). But for a brief moment, Walter is at peace with himself as a man, even if it in an intoxicated state of fantasy.

TEXT	REFERENCE	NOTES
Mama: "Once upon a time freedom used to be life – now it's money. […] You something new, boy. In my time we was worried about not being lynched […]." (p. 74)	(pp. 74–75)	Family means generations – people and values from different periods clashing as the young reject the old and the old struggle to share their wisdom with the young. Both Walter and Beneatha represent a new kind of African-American (Ruth less so). Walter lacks his father's strength and energy, and we can see him as the beaten descendant of people who have been abused and oppressed for too long. He fails to understand the sacrifices made by his mother's generation to ensure that he had a home to live in. His struggles, despite his materialism and obsession with money, have more to do with frustrated pride and a weak aggressiveness born of impotence and anger. Beneatha is also a very new phenomenon, but the polar opposite of her brother. Where he is negative and selfish, Beneatha is wide-eyed and curious. He has dreams, she has plans. Walter only thinks in terms of money, while Beneatha wants to express herself. Their mother is baffled by her own children, displaying another aspect of family dynamics, with the tension between generations.

TEXT	REFERENCE	NOTES
"The character who emerges as the most compelling in this production is Ruth Younger. Starletta DuPois understates the conflicting emotions Ruth suffers as she realizes a gulf has opened between her and her husband, Walter Lee, and reveals the distance between her and his mother, Lena, and his sister, Beneatha. The result is a full flowering of a character who in most productions remains a kind of blotting paper for the emotional outpourings of the others. Miss DuPois's exultant call for the furniture movers to come up to the Younger apartment in the last scene releases more pent up joy than in any production I know of."[10]	(excerpt from a review of a stage production of *A Raisin in the Sun* published in the *New York Times*)	The play begins with Ruth, and we can end this section on family by looking at a reaction to the character of Ruth in a review of a 1986 production of the play. The reviewer highlights very important aspects of Ruth's character and role within the family. The description of Ruth as character usually portrayed as "blotting paper" (Löschpapier) is extremely interesting because it shows the depths of the figure. She is of course the woman who has to receive her husband's endless abuse and complaints, like blotting paper receives ink, and she tolerates her sister-in-law's craziness and her mother-in-law's total control. But while she may be quieter than Beneatha and Walter, who are both quite histrionic, passionate and emotionally expressive characters, Ruth has several moments of great emotional intensity during the play. What is mentioned here is her joy at the prospect of being able to leave the apartment and move to a new home. We should also remember, dealing here with the themes of family and gender issues, that it is Ruth who is struggling with the idea of an abortion, a very real and deeply traumatic prospect for a woman who loves her family yet knows she can't afford to handle another child. She is completely alone with this devastating situation: Walter runs away and Lena's disapproval is as biblical as could be expected.

10 https://www.nytimes.com/1986/08/15/theater/stage-at-roundabout-a-raisin-in-the-sun.html

Dreams, hopes, ambitions – the future

Of all the themes addressed in the play, this is maybe the most ambiguous. The race-related topics are crucial and interesting, but they are at heart pretty simple: **It's irrational and wrong to judge people by the colour of their skin**. Injustice and oppression harm individuals, families and communities. These are important things which need to be addressed and constantly reaffirmed.

Dreams nearly ruin the family

But the matter of all these intangible, future-based ideas – dreams, hope, faith – is much less clear-cut. Without dreams, Walter Lee feels half-dead, crushed and neglected, less than a man. But diving headlong into his dreams nearly ruins the family – to chase his dreams he takes the money and entrusts it to a shady character (Willie Harris) who immediately steals it. Dreams are a luxury Ruth cannot afford: She has too much work to do and too much here-and-now to worry about. The future is what seems to occupy most of Beneatha's attention. And the absence of a future and of hope for the boy Travis is a heart-breaking factor for the Younger family.

→ **Dreams** are important, but they can be dangerous as well: Ruth is eminently practical, she doesn't have the opportunity to dream, she has too much reality to deal with. Walter on the other hand is only a dreamer who lacks the discipline and knowledge to tackle his dreams. Beneatha is also a dreamer, but she is educated and intelligent and has more focussed, realistic ideas than Walter.

→ A key scene for the relationship Walter has to the **future**, rather than to his wild dreams of wealth and success, comes on page 73. "Sometimes it's like I can see the future stretched out in front of me – just plain as day. The future, Mama. Hanging over there at the edge of my days. Just waiting for me – a big, looming blank space – full of *nothing*." He immediately afterwards begins talking about money again, but this speech gives us an insight into the despair at the heart of his character, the despair which drives his anger, bitterness, frustration and aggression. Walter's dreams are crazy fantasies of wealth, but his future, the future he sees for himself, is a dark, hopeless place.

The apartment as a symbol of the decay of the family

No future here

The apartment and its ageing furnishings are described at the beginning of the play using the words *care, love, hope, taste* and *pride*. But this refers to what it was. What it is, is tired and depressed (see p. 23). The apartment and its old and worn-out contents are strong and constant symbols of what has happened to the Younger family. It is being held together by Mama's strength and Ruth's work, but it can't carry on much longer. Just like the furniture is described as having to "*fight to show itself*" under things which have "*finally come to be more important than the upholstery*", and objects have been moved "*to disguise the worn places*", the weariness and depression in the Younger family can no longer be ignored or overlooked. Ruth's exhaustion, Walter's bitterness and frustration, the lack of perspectives for Travis and the lack of space and opportunity for Beneatha – these are all major themes in the play which are embedded from the very beginning in the poverty and squalor of their environment.

This is what makes the new house in Clybourne Park so very important. It represents new hope, new beginnings and a healthy re-energising of the family's very spirit.

Another point to remember is the matter of light. When the apartment is described at the opening of the play, we are told: "*The sole natural light the family may enjoy in the course of a day is only that which fights its way through this little window*" (p. 24). The symbolism is again not hard to unwrap. This is a dark place, and with no light there is no hope.

Race and identity

TEXT	REFERENCE	NOTES
Lindner: "I want you to believe me when I tell you that race prejudice simply doesn't enter into it. It is a matter of the people of Clybourne Park believing, rightly or wrongly, as I say, that for the happiness of all concerned that our Negro families are happier when they live in their *own* communities." (p. 118); "What do you think you are going to gain by moving into a neighbourhood where you just aren't wanted [...]." (p. 119)	(pp. 113–119)	The racial themes dominate in *A Raisin in the Sun*. The central conflict, the dynamic core of the plot, is the attempt by the white residents of Clybourne Park, as represented by Karl Lindner, to buy off the Youngers and thus prevent a black family from moving into their middle-class white neighbourhood. Lindner is a harmless-seeming man, unwilling to say plainly what is actually going on. Beneatha is the first to realise what is happening, but eventually Walter and Ruth also understand what he is trying to say. The idea of segregation is that people of different races or ethnicities should live with their own kind and not mingle or share neighbourhoods with others. It was a fact of life in the South, one reason why so many African-Americans moved northwards during the Great Migrations of the early 20th century. The segregation we see here is mixed up with fears that having black neighbours may lower the value of the white residents' properties; but also, as Lindner

3.5 Notes on themes

TEXT	REFERENCE	NOTES
		alludes to in a quite sinister manner, there is a threat of violence. He suggests that some people in the area might be so unhappy about black families moving in that they may start to attack them, even using bombs.
(1) Asagai, talking to Beneatha: "you said [...] (*He imitates her*) 'Mr. Asagai – I want very much to talk with you. About Africa. You see, Mr. Asagai, I am looking for my *identity*!'" (2) Asagai: "Assimilationism is so popular in your country." (3) George: "Here we go! A lecture on the African past! On our Great West African Heritage! [...] (*Nastily*) Let's face it, baby, your heritage is nothing but a bunch of raggedy-assed spirituals and some grass huts! (4) [Beneatha and Asagai talk]	(1) p. 62 (2) p. 63 (3) p. 81 (4) pp. 131–137	Aside from this central theme of racism, we have the triangle of Beneatha and the two men courting her: the "assimilationist", middle-class George Murchison, and the more globally aware and intellectually sophisticated Joseph Asagai. These two men present conflicting and very different images of black culture. Asagai believes in and works towards independence for the peoples of Africa from the colonialist powers. Beneatha is fascinated by the issue. And George struggles with the realities exposed by Walter having lost their money. And George displays nothing but contempt for any kind of positive black identity: He rejects Walter's greeting of "black brother" and his dismissal of everything African is probably the most racist statement we see in the entire play, including anything said by Karl Lindner. The second conversation between Beneatha and Asagai is an extremely important example of how the themes of black struggles are seen in different lights. The Nigerian has a completely different concept of time, hope and the nature of the struggle than does Beneatha, whose linear concept of time and fatalistic view is in that moment dominated by her depression and fury at her brother's stupidity in having lost all their money (including the money which was intended for her education).

TEXT	REFERENCE	NOTES
Walter: "That is just what is wrong with the colored woman in this world… Don't understand about building their men up and making 'em feel like they some-body. Like they can do something." Ruth: (*Drily, but to hurt*) "There are colored men who do things." Walter: "No thanks to the colored wom-an."	(p. 34)	Walter Lee provides a third example, the most conflicted and frustrated of them all. The play begins with him attacking his wife (and all other black women) for not providing adequate support to him (and all other black men). His frustration with his own failures has been poisoned and has become in a way a hatred of being black. Later, drunk and enthralled by the Nige-rian energy of Beneatha's music, dancing and clothing, Walter thoroughly em-braces his blackness and his African-ness.
(1) [Mama talking about her husband Walter] (2) [Walter learns about Willie Harris' betrayal and theft of the money]	(1) pp. 44–46 (2) pp. 125–129	We also have two other examples of black men, neither of whom we see on stage: "Big" Walter Younger, Lena's husband and Walter Lee and Beneatha's father, who is described to us by Lena in respect-ful tones and embodies a strong, tough ideal of manhood; and Willie Harris, the predator.
Beneatha: "[…] the only people in the world who are more snobbish than rich white people are rich colored people."	(pp. 49–50)	As we have seen with George Murchi-son's racism towards Africa, there are complex internal struggles within the broader spectrum of white / black racism. Beneatha highlights here the difficulties of reconciling racial identity with money.

The philosophy of *A Raisin in the Sun*

Role model "Mama" Lena: love and hope

A few key lines in the play suggest Hansberry's underlying **thoughts about life and how to live it** – her philosophy, roughly. The most significant, considering how the conflicts in the play are resolved – with the Younger family staying together – and what we know of her own beliefs, is probably "There is *always* something left to love" (p. 145), spoken by "Mama" Lena Younger, who is almost certainly Lorraine Hansberry's favourite character in the play. Lena provides the foundation for the family, the solid basis on which they can all rest. She can also be seen as an anchor, holding them together as they are blown around by circumstance.

This positive **message of love** contains the sense of perseverance which Asagai also tries to explain to Beneatha when she is so upset at Walter having lost their money. She complains that the world is full of "crooks and thieves and just plain idiots" (p. 133), but Asagai argues that that is not where life stops; it continues. The efforts to become free and to attain independence and dignity continue. The hope which is inherent in both his argument and Mama's philosophy of the eternal power of love are at the core of Hansberry's intentions with the play. **There is a message of strength under the despair and poverty and struggles**.

3.6 Style and language

SUMMARY

- → Because it is a stage play, written in a specific format, *A Raisin in the Sun* contains two distinct kinds of language: stage directions and dramatic lines.
- → We will also look in this chapter at the unusual, creative use of language, and the Yoruba language of West Africa, which plays a small but significant role in the relationship between Beneatha and Joseph.

The language of plays, scripts and screenplays

In prose (the kind of language used in short stories or novels) there will usually be at least two different kinds of language: the **language used to describe the world** and what is going on, and then **the language used by the characters** when they talk to one another.

Plays are similar, but they are more formally structured: there are stage directions (the world and what is going on in it) and there are lines (what the characters say to one another).

Stage directions

The performance of the actors

The first kind of language is primarily functional. It has to provide **concrete information and guidelines** for the people who will be turning the words on the page into a living, breathing stage performance. But it has another, more complex purpose. It also has to suggest tone and nuance: How is Beneatha feeling? Is her response sarcastic? Is Ruth tired, sad, angry, impatient, happy, or irritated? The combination of theatrical language, spoken lines and the context can create strong impressions for anyone planning a performance of the play.

The stage directions will tell us what is happening: Ruth is standing in the living room doing the ironing or the laundry, for example, or Beneatha is talking on the telephone. But these very specific directions can be enhanced or fleshed out with more subtle nuances which can add to our **understanding of the characters' personalities, behaviour and roles**.

An example of technical and suggestive stage directions

Create an emotional impression

For an example of how stage directions can be suggestive, and serve both a literary and a technical function, look at **the end of Act I Scene 2**, when Mama and Ruth are waiting to hear Walter's reaction to the news that Ruth is planning to get an abortion. The stage direction says "*Pause. The silence shouts*" (p. 75). The pause is a technical direction – the actors are to wait before speaking the next line. But what do we make of "*the silence shouts*"? That is a message to the director and to the actors about how to use their art **to imply the tension and stress** of this very short moment in time while we wait for Walter's reaction. There is no technical advice here: The performers and the director are being told by the author that they must create an emotional and psychological impression here.

Technical stage directions

The stage directions do need a little more explanation, though. Certain technical terms are used for stage directions, and it is important that people writing plays, scripts or screenplays stick to the formal, technical language. Here are brief explanations of some of the terms used in the text of *A Raisin in the Sun*.

TERM	EXPLANATION
Enter	A character comes onto the stage and joins the action.
Exit	A character leaves the stage.
Stage left / right	Refers to the actor's left or right when they face the audience.
Curtain	The end of the performance, referring to the curtain which is lowered or drawn across the stage.

The actors' lines

The words spoken by the actors – the lines – are more malleable: They can be shaped like clay, depending on the attributes and intentions of the actors and the skills and aims of the director. These are the most explicit manifestations of what the playwright intends to say: **These are the words the audience hears**, embedded in the interpretations of the stage directions and the guiding vision of the production.

For our purposes, the lines for the actors can be treated like any other kind of **text to be analysed and interpreted**. We can read them as we would read any other literary text and examine them on their own merits.

Creative use of language in *A Raisin in the Sun*

Lorraine Hansberry's *A Raisin in the Sun* is written in a black dialect. The characters use a different figurative language: Beneatha's speech for example is much closer to Standard American English than her mother's.

"slubborn"

There is a playful and inventive use of language – made-up words like "slubborn-ness" (p. 29), "ghetto-itis" (p. 60) and "tooken" (p. 141), for example, none of which exist in the English language. Yet these words manage to tell us quite a lot: "slubborn-ness" is related to slovenly, meaning careless, untidy or dirty in appearance or habits. But it also suggests "stubborn" – determined not to change one's attitude or opinion. The combination creates an ideal adjective for describing the mess created by a strong-willed group of people living in a small shared space in relative poverty, like the Youngers, or even more suitably, the kind of chaos created by a 10-year old boy like Travis.

"ghetto-itis"

"ghetto-itis" is the word Beneatha uses to explain (or rather, avoid explaining) to Joseph Asagai why she is so upset when he comes to their apartment (p. 60). The suffix –itis is a medical term, used in Latin but originally Greek, which means "the inflammation of an organ"[11] or, more generally "a disease of"[12] some part of the body. But it has a figurative, colloquial meaning as well, defined as "too much of" or "too much interest in"[13]. The OALD uses the example "World Cup-itis" to illustrate how a single issue (the football World Cup) can be so dominant that **you feel** sick of it – like an illness. Here in *Raisin*, Beneatha is using the suffix to express how she and the family are miserable from having to live in the ghetto. The poverty, the cramped living conditions, the huge rats which provide the only entertainment for the children – it's all become too much, it's like a disease, an illness, a condition they are suffering from.

"tooken"

"tooken" (p. 141) is another playful (albeit bitter) and knowingly ignorant use of language. Walter means "taken" – he is talking about the takers and those who get taken from – but his bitterness has him playing a role, expressing his diminished sense of self-worth through a theatrical display of the kind of ignorance he believes society and the world expects from a black man. We know that Walter is an eloquent man. We have heard him using language that

---

11 https://www.merriam-webster.com/dictionary/-itis
12 Oxford Advanced Learner's Dictionary.
13 Ibid.

rises and exalts, visionary language, also language which is precise and cutting. But he chooses here **to mock himself** and his shame by making an intentional mistake.

Yoruba

The Yoruba are **a tribe in western Africa**, historically linked to Nigeria, where they currently make up roughly 20% of the country's population. Yoruba is also **the name of the tribal language**.

Slave trade

The Yoruba, their culture and language were brought to the Americas as part of the slave trade, and the Yoruba language has left its traces across the Caribbean. The original Yoruba culture, like most others hit by the slave trade, has not survived intact in the West, but it has left echoes and adapted forms. Slave trafficked cultures like those of West Africa cannot be described like immigrant cultures (for example, the Polish or Irish Catholic immigrants to the USA in the early 20th century) – there was nothing remotely voluntary about their transition to America, and no hope at all of anything resembling an American Dream. But like immigrant cultures, trafficked or slave cultures can leave traces on, or rather, can add elements to, a melting pot culture like that of the USA.

Joseph Asagai, the Nigerian student in *Raisin*, introduces himself to Mama as being Yoruba, which confuses the old woman, who had thought he was Nigerian (although she couldn't recall that name either). He uses **Yoruba words** when Beneatha tries on the robe he has brought her, and he uses a Yoruba name for her ("Alaiyo"). This name means "She For Whom Bread Alone Is Not Enough". This name is a clear reference to a quotation from the Bible (see the chapter in this study guide on Origins and Sources for more on this, p. 40).

3.7 Interpretations

SUMMARY

→ *A Raisin in the Sun* tells a clear and unambiguous story. There is not too much room for speculation about the themes and motives of the play and its characters. The play should be interpreted in the context of its own contemporary background and against the history of black people inside and out of Africa.

→ Efforts to expand upon (the "Raisin Cycle") or adapt the play to other media (the film) have remained close to the tone and message of Hansberry's original play.

Background

As discussed in the chapter in this study guide on the play's Contemporary Background (see chapter 2.2, p. 12), *Raisin* is inspired by real things which were **close to Hansberry's life**. The author does use metaphors and symbols – the weary state of the family's apartment is one, Mama's little plant is another – but the play as a whole is more realist and concerned with existing issues. The play is not an allegory or a poetic effort to talk about something other than what it seems to be.

Black history

Interpreting the play and its success and relevance requires students to know a little about **Hansberry's history** (discussed elsewhere in this study guide), and the situation facing **African-Americans in the US** (specifically in the big cities) in the 1950s. Hansberry was a civil rights activist, and she and her play should be seen as belonging to **the civil rights movement** which was about to enter its most historically prominent, critical phase with the rise (and assassinations) of Martin Luther King Jr and Malcolm X.

Africanism

The issue of Africa and African heritage and identity had come to prominence during the cultural movement known as the **Harlem Renaissance in the 1920s and 1930s**. While many artists and writers from that period slipped into obscurity, the ideas they were exploring were important and remained fertile ground for black artists for decades to come. One of these issues was a creative, artistic treatment of **Pan-Africanism**, a movement intended to unify the global descendants of all people coming from Africa throughout history. This issue had interested Hansberry on a political level, and the character of Joseph Asagai shows us how important and strong the idea and appeal of **African heritage and identity** was for her. His presence is strong and cheerful, and he inspires Beneatha's energy (as well as Walter Lee's visions) in a way which his dramatic and thematic opposite, George Murchison, simply can't. Hansberry's attitude towards "real" Africa is evident in the positive example Asagai represents of a confident, culturally sophisticated intellectual: This character and the ideas he embodies are significant, and when talking about *Raisin*, students must bear in mind how important the issue of Africa was to Hansberry and her contemporary audiences.

Adaptations

Screenplay by Hansberry

The play was **adapted for the cinema in 1961** with a screenplay written by Lorraine Hansberry. Hansberry stayed very close to her original play, adapting some scenes so that the dialogue could take place in other settings, thus making use of the greater opportunities provided by film.

Director

Director of the film adaption was **Daniel Petrie** (1920–2004). *Raisin* was the most famous and significant film he was to make: He also directed B movies in the 1980s (*Fort Apache, the Bronx*, 1981 and *Cocoon 2: The Return*, 1988) and worked a lot for television.

The producers were **Philip Rose and David Susskind**. Rose was a Broadway theatrical producer known for his interest in material that tackled social issues. He was deeply opposed to racism and injustice and used his position as a producer to help writers and artists fight against ignorance and discrimination. Susskind was a more prominent celebrity at the time and was also known for his commitment to progressive issues of civil rights and social injustice. Producers

The cast of the 1961 film adaptation included almost all the same actors who were in the original stage production. Cast

ROLE	ACTOR
Walter Lee Younger	**Sidney Poitier** (*1927) works less these days as an actor (he is also an activist and diplomat), but during the 1960s and 1970s he was one of the most prominent, successful and decorated African-American actors working in cinema. He has won and been nominated for Oscars many times and was nominated for two major awards for his performance in the film adaptation of *Raisin*.
Ruth Younger	**Ruby Dee** (1922–2014) was an actor, poet and civil rights activist. She played Ruth in the original stage production of *Raisin*. She also appeared in films by Spike Lee (*Do the Right Thing*, 1989) and Ridley Scott (*American Gangster*, 2007)
"Mama" Lena Younger	**Claudia McNeil** (1917–1993) was nominated for a Golden Globe award for her role in the film.
Beneatha Younger	**Diana Sands** (1934–1973)
Travis Younger	**Stephen Perry** (*1952)
Mark Lindner[14]	**John Fiedler** (1925–2005) worked as an actor for over 50 years and appeared in more than 190 films and TV shows.

14 Note the name change here. In the play, this character is called Karl. It's not known why this change was made.

ROLE	ACTOR
Joseph Asagai	**Ivan Dixon** (1931–2008) was a prominent civil rights activist as well as being a popular actor (in particular for his role in the TV sitcom *Hogan's Heroes* 1965–1971).
George Murchison	**Louis Gossett Jr** (*1936) had his first screen role in *Raisin* (he was also in the stage production). He went on to have a long and successful career for decades, appearing in dozens and dozens of films across many different genres. He has also worked extensively in television.
Bobo	**Joel Fluellen** (1907–1990) had been an actor since the 1930s, and so was along with Roy Glenn the most experienced member of the cast of *Raisin*.
Willie Harris	**Roy Glenn** (1914–1971) also began his career in film in the 1930s. He also appeared with Sidney Poitier in *Guess Who's Coming to Dinner* (1967).

Additional scenes

The film was successful and popular. It remains very close to the original stage play, and often feels as theatrical as a stage play, with characters speaking towards the camera in uninterrupted monologues. Hansberry rewrote some scenes to allow the setting to change (for example, when the family goes to visit the house they want to buy, or when Lena comes to find Walter Lee in the bar), and **some scenes are included to illustrate Walter's frustration and depression** (scenes of him working or sitting in the bar). There are also a couple of new scenes not included in the play, such as a **meeting between Walter, Willie and Bobo in the bar**. The information and plot elements in this particular scene are not new: Instead of finding things out in a roundabout way through conversations between Walter and his family, we instead see here the original conversations. This again allows the film to provide more variety of setting and scenery than the original stage play can provide, and it also lets us see Willie Harris, who is vital to the plot of the play but is never seen in the original.

Sidney Poitier as Walter Lee (1961)

Other adaptations

The play has been adapted for other media, including a successful 2008 film version starring rapper/producer Sean Combs as Walter Lee, which premiered at the prestigious *Sundance Film Festival*, and as a radio play for the British BBC in 1996 and again in 2016.

The "Raisin Cycle"

Clybourne Park (2010)

As mentioned in an earlier chapter in this study guide (see p. 38), the playwright Bruce Norris had written a play called *Clybourne Park* in 2010 which expanded on the world of *A Raisin in the Sun*. The play is in two acts, the first set just before the Younger family move to their new house – **we learn a lot more about the white residents of the neighbourhood**; the Korean War (1950–1953) is also a theme, as is suicide. The second act takes place 50 years later. Clybourne Park is by this time an all-black neighbourhood in the process of being gentrified: Young white people are trying to buy the old houses and tear them down to build new luxury housing.

Beneatha's Place (2013)

In 2013 British actor and playwright Kwame Kwei-Armah wrote a play called *Beneatha's Place*, which follows **Beneatha Younger's life as she and Joseph Asagai move to Nigeria** and she later becomes Dean at a Californian university. Kwei-Armah called his play the third in the "Raisin Cycle".

Fundamental themes

The existence of these two plays is proof of the lasting **importance of Hansberry's play**. This is not like a film studio deciding to make another *Star Wars* movie to cash in on a pop cultural goldmine: These are two artists who were evidently so moved, intrigued and inspired by the characters and themes of *A Raisin in the Sun* that they felt the need to further explore them. And of equal importance is the fact that these two other authors both moved their focus onto the world of today: So instead of being an exercise in nostalgia or a mere tribute to **a great work of another era**, the works by Norris and Kwei-Armah prove how important and fundamental Hansberry's themes really are.

Macklemore's mistake

White American rapper Macklemore (Benjamin Haggerty) mentions *A Raisin in the Sun* in the song *Growing Up (Sloane's Song)* from his 2016 album *The Unruly Mess I've Made*. The song lyrics are in the form of a letter to his new baby daughter (Sloane) in which he gives her random advice on life. The song contains the line: "Read Langston Hughes, I suggest A Raisin in the Sun"[15]. At the time, Macklemore was an exceedingly popular music artist star, and many fans, musicians and journalists **immediately spotted his mistake**[16]. The title of the play was taken from a poem by Langston Hughes – which Macklemore's mistake implies that he knew – but the author was of course Lorraine Hansberry.

Though this mistake was unfortunate for Macklemore, **we can see here that the play has had a lasting influence** and that its legacy continues. Macklemore, as a white American product of modern pop culture, considers it an important enough work of American literature to include it in his lessons for his baby. Strangely, this blunder tells us quite a bit about how the play has come to be interpreted in the 21st century: as an important, vital work of anti-racism and enlightenment for white audiences about the lives and struggles of black people in America.

---

15 Songwriter: Ben Haggerty / Tyler Williams / Ed Sheeran / Ryan Lewis / Joshua Rawlings / Owuor Arunga / Joshua Karp. © Kobalt Music Publishing Ltd. See https://www.youtube.com/watch?v=6mhtJduoCZ0

16 http://www.mtv.com/news/2233606/macklemore-a-raisin-in-the-sun-fail/

4. RECEPTION

SUMMARY

A Raisin in the Sun was a critical success and has maintained a good reputation since it was first performed. It is considered to be one of the first, and certainly one of the most important plays about the modern African-American experience, as well as being a fine drama about family dynamics.

Success

"Black playwright Charles Gordone, author of *No Place to Be Somebody* [...] considered Hansberry's 1959 *A Raisin in the Sun* [...] to be the initiating work in modern Black theatre."[17]

"The events of every passing year add resonance to *A Raisin in the Sun* [...]. It is as if history is conspiring to make the play a classic."[18]

"It was 25 years ago that a 28-year-old black woman from this city changed American theater forever with her first produced play. The woman was Lorraine Hansberry, and the play, of course, was *'A Raisin in the Sun'*. [...] this seminal play – which sparked the growth of the black theater movement in the 1960's [...]."[19]

---

17 White, Edmund: *Genet*. London: Chatto & Windus, 1993, p. 308.

18 From J-R. Bruckner's New York Times review of the 1986 production, quoted in Nemiroff's Introduciton to the play, p. 5. See also https://www.nytimes.com/1986/08/15/theater/stage-at-roundabout-a-raisin-in-the-sun.html for the complete review.

19 Rich, Frank: *Theater: Raisin in the Sun Anniversary in Chicago* (1983). https://www.nytimes.com/1983/10/05/theater/theater-raisin-in-sun-anniversary-in-chicago.html

Raisin has been recognised as both **a good and an important play**. Good because it entertainingly and interestingly tells a story with engaging characters, with both emotional and intellectual rewards for the audience, and important because it is **a landmark in the development of African-American literature**. Both of these claims about the play can be supported by the continuing success it has enjoyed. Not only has it been in its history adapted into a successful film, it has also continued to be produced on stage and adapted for radio and television. Other authors have written sequels. **People still want to see, stage and discuss this play**. This very real and existing legacy is proof enough of the durability and relevance of Hansberry's play.

Continuing success

Historically, the play is important because it was **the first ever play by an African-American woman to be staged on Broadway**. The specific issues of how race affected the play's reception will be looked at in the next section (p. 109).

This quotation from a 1983 review of the play by Frank Rich provides an excellent summary of why the play has been so successful and why it is significant:

> "Taking her title from Langston Hughes's poem '*Harlem*,' Miss Hansberry forced both blacks and whites to re-examine the deferred dreams of black America. She asked blacks to reconsider how those dreams might be defined; she demanded that whites not impede the fulfillment of those dreams for one more second. And she posed all her concerns in a work that portrayed a black family with a greater realism and complexity than had ever been previously seen on an American stage. A writer of unlimited compassion, Miss Hansberry believed that all people must be measured, as she put it, by both their 'hills and valleys.'"[20]

Why the play has been so successful

20 Ibid.

Civil rights

The same reviewer, Frank Rich, also highlights Hansberry's important position in the **history of the civil rights movement**, both as an activist and as an artist with an unusually acute perception:

> "[...] she saw history whole: Her play encompasses everything from the rise of black nationalism in the United States and Africa to the advent of black militancy to the specific dimensions of the black woman's liberation movement."[21]

The reviewer highlights Walter Lee as the dramatic focus:

The figure of Walter Lee Younger

> "But Miss Hansberry's real drama is the battle for the soul and identity of Walter Lee Younger, the family's son. Walter, 35, is a chauffeur who wants to get rich by opening a liquor store. Without quite realizing it, he oppresses his wife, Ruth, a domestic, and mocks the ambitions of his 20-year-old sister, Beneatha, a fledgling activist and medical student. "I got me a dream," says Walter early in the play – but his dream is not to be confused with Dr. King's. What he wants is 'things,' and, as he tells his horrified mother, Lena, he no longer regards money merely as a passport to freedom but as the essence of life. In this sense, Walter is not just a black victim of white racism but also a victim of a materialistic American dream that can enslave men or women of any race.[22]

---

21 Ibid.
22 Ibid.

Ambiguous responses

The Introduction to the play, by Robert Nemiroff, draws our attention to some of the contemporary reactions to the racial identity of the author, the characters, and the setting. This is a fascinating and difficult topic. The basic idea, as explained in the text quoted from Ossie Davis (pp. 8–9), is that a certain kind of white audience in America, and he suggests this is the majority of those who responded positively to the play, wanted to claim it as a universal statement of humanity, a play about how people everywhere just want to be people, how we all want the same things in life, we all want to be happy with our families. But **this colour-blind reaction**, it is argued, ignores the realities of the African-American experience in a white-dominated, racist society like the USA. A 60-year old white woman will not have had the same experiences in life as "Mama" Lena Younger has had, even if the two come from the same economic class. A frustrated young white man will feel very different pressures from those experienced by Walter Lee Younger. **Race matters**: Only the privileged – white people – will ever argue that it doesn't. In the same way that money is only a toy to those who have too much of it, in the caste-like social hierarchies of race, **racism is only invisible to those who sit at the top.**

A *universal* statement of humanity?

An essay written for *Harvard University's Journal of Modern Drama* focuses on the conflict between the "universality" and the "particularity" of the play, and how complex the issue of race is[23]. By "universality", the author, Robin Bernstein, explains, he is referring to the responses by white critics (and audiences) like this one:

Audience

23 Bernstein, Robin: *Inventing a fishbowl: White supremacy and the critical reception of Lorraine Hansberry's A raisin in the sun*. 1999. https://dash.harvard.edu/handle/1/3659695

> "A Negro wrote this show. It is played, with one exception, by Negroes. Half the audiences here are Negroes. Even so, it isn't written for Negroes ... It's a show about people, white or colored."[24]

The "particularity" the author refers is the opposite of the universality – the idea that this is not a play about "people", it is **a play about specifically African-American people**.

Universal or specifically black?

Hansberry herself is quoted in the essay in response to this issue. When asked by an interviewer about the universality versus particularity of her play and its appeal, she says:

> "I hadn't noticed the contradiction because I'd always been under the impression that Negroes are people."[25]

This is a response to the thematic issue of **black and white audiences and responses**, but she also talks about her technical, literary approach, which also refuses to acknowledge the conflict:

> "One of the most sound ideas in dramatic writing is that in order to create the universal, you must pay great attention to the specific."[26]

---

24 Ibid p. 16.
25 Ibid. p. 16.
26 Ibid. pp. 16–17.

5. MATERIALS

Lorraine Hansberry and Bobby Kennedy (1963)

On May 24 1963 Robert ("Bobby") Kennedy, the Attorney General of the US[27] and brother to the current president, John F Kennedy, organised a meeting with various African-American thinkers, celebrities, artists and cultural figures.

The Baldwin-Kennedy-meeting

The aim of the meeting was to discuss ways to improve race relations within the US. The group of invitees included primarily novelist James Baldwin, activist and singer Harry Belafonte, the singer and activist Lena Horne, Martin Luther King Jr's senior advisor Clarence Benjamin Jones, and several others. Lorraine Hansberry was included in the group. She was 33 at the time, and it was a year before her death.

In his unfinished notes to a major book project with the working title *Remember This House*[28], James Baldwin recalls an interaction between Hansberry and Bobby Kennedy at this meeting. An infamous photograph of a white policeman standing on the neck of a black woman lying (see p. 112) on the ground had caused a great deal of shock and outrage, as had numerous reports and documents of brutality by whites and the police against black people during those most tumultuous years of the civil rights movement. Hansberry confronted Kennedy, and Baldwin, who knew her well and admired her greatly, was deeply impressed by her authority and

---

27 The chief lawyer representing the federal government of the United States.
28 The notes for this project were used by Haitian filmmaker Raoul Peck as the basis for his documentary film (and accompanying book of the same title) *I Am not Your Negro* (2016). The passage here is quoted from the book: Peck and Baldwin, *I Am Not Your Negro*. London: Penguin Modern Classics, 2017. pp 42–44.

Policemen restrain a woman on the ground during racial protest marches in Birmingham (May 6, 1963). © picture alliance/AP

strength when facing up to one of the most powerful white men in the US.

"We would like," said Lorraine, "from you, a moral commitment."
He looked insulted – seemed to feel that he had been wasting his time.
Well Lorraine sat still, watching all the while…
She looked at Bobby Kennedy, who, perhaps for the first time, looked at her.

"But I am very worried," she said, "about the state of the civilization which produced that photograph of the white cop standing on that Negro woman's neck in Birmingham."
The, she smiled.
And I am glad that she was not smiling at me.
"Goodbye, Mr. Attorney General," she said, and turned and walked out of the room.[29]

I Am Not Your Negro (2017)

Hansberry and the Town Hall forum (1964)

The Town Hall forum in New York City was conceived and established as a platform for discussion between white liberals and black activists about topics related to the civil rights movement.

White liberals and black activists

It was supported by the Association of Artists for Freedom, an organisation of black performers and writers including the actor Sidney Poitier (who had starred as Walter Lee in the Broadway production and film adaptation of *A Raisin in the Sun*) and author James Baldwin, a good friend of Lorraine Hansberry.

Hansberry gave a speech to the forum in 1964. She had been raised by her parents to be socially conscious and politically active, and her ideas and principles had been further sharpened and focussed by her early time in New York with the prominent activists and leaders, W.E.B. Du Bois and Paul Robeson. By 1964 Hansberry had become fiercer in her commitment to the civil rights movement, and was growing more impatient with the inability of white liberals to accept and support the African-American demands for equal rights and fair treatment: "Negroes are so angry and white people

29 Ibid., p. 43–44.

are so confused and sensitive to criticism," she wrote soon after giving the speech[30]. The momentum of the civil rights movement in the late 1950s and early to mid-1960s was becoming more urgent and more impassioned as the powers that be – white politicians, the police, structural racism – fought back ever more violently against the movement. Hansberry's speech in 1964 addressed her feelings about this urgency and specifically looked at her background (her parents' activism).

"I am of a generation of Negroes that comes after a whole lot of other generations and my father, for instance, who was, you know, real "American" type American: successful businessman, very civic-minded and so forth; was the sort of American who put a great deal of money, a great deal of his really extraordinary talents and a great deal of passion into everything that we say is the American way of going after goals. That is to say that he moved his family into a restricted area where no Negroes were supposed to live and then proceeded to fight the case in the courts all the way to the Supreme Court of the United States. And this cost a great deal of money. It involved the assistance of NAACP attorneys and so on and this is the way of struggling that everyone says is the proper way to do and it eventually resulted in a decision against restrictive covenants which is very famous, Hansberry v. Lee. And that was very much applauded.

But the problem is that Negroes are just as segregated in the city of Chicago now as they were then [laughter] and my father died a disillusioned exile in another country."

30 All quotations from http://americanradioworks.publicradio.org/features/blackspeech/lhansberry.html

Hansberry v. Lee

Hansberry refers to her father here, and what he represents, as an example of the traditional, system-sanctioned way of getting things done, but her bitter conclusion is that it just doesn't work for black Americans. Following the rules and doing things the way middle-class white people would is insufficient.

She argues that when white people in 1964 complain about the increasing radicalism of African-American communities and activists they seem unaware of the fact that for literally three hundred years black people in America have been struggling against brutal institutional racism of various degrees, using all the instruments at their disposal. If America's own legal system and social order, the very fabric of American society, can't help, as in the case of her father, then what is left but radical action?

"It isn't as if we got up today and said, you know, 'what can we do to irritate America?' [laughter] you know. It's because that since 1619, Negroes have tried every method of communication, of transformation of their situation from petition to the vote, everything. We've tried it all. There isn't anything that hasn't been exhausted."[31]

Unwillingness of white liberal Americans

She spoke about the increased accusations against radical black activists and thinkers that they were being too hasty, too impatient, too radical – these accusations coming from white liberals, people she and other African-American activists had hoped would be on their side in the struggle for civil rights and the fight against injustice and inequality.

"And now the charge of impatience is simply unbearable. I would like to submit that the problem is that, yes, there is a problem about

31 Ibid.

white liberals. … The problem is we have to find some way with these dialogues to show and to encourage the white liberal to stop being a liberal and become an American radical. … The basic organization of American society is the thing that has Negroes in the situation that they are in and never let us lose sight of it. … This is why we want the dialogue, to explain that to you, you see. It isn't a question of patriotism and loyalty. My brother fought for this country, my grandfather before that and so on and that's all a lot of nonsense when we criticize. The point is that we have a different viewpoint because, you know, we've been kicked in the face so often and the vantage point of Negroes is entirely different and these are some of the things we're trying to say."[32]

The big issue here, the problem the Town Hall forum was established to address, was the issue that had been very much present in a lot of James Baldwin's writings, too: the inability or unwillingness of white liberal Americans to accept the independence and validity of African-American experience and agency. Hansberry was angry at being accused of impatience by white liberals because she understood that they wanted to run the show and dictate the pace. And the humiliation of having to be grateful to yet more white saviours was impossible to accept for this generation of black civil rights activists. The desperate, violent struggles for freedom, justice and fundamental civic rights in this era were fought by black activists against not just the oppressive authorities of a deeply racist, white supremacist society, but against their own alleged allies in these struggles, the privileged white liberals of America.

32 Ibid.

6. SAMPLE EXAM QUESTIONS AND ANSWERS

Die Zahl der Sternchen bezeichnet das Anforderungsniveau der jeweiligen Aufgabe.

Here are some sample essay questions and responses. The number of stars indicates the level of difficulty of the task.

Task 1 **

Dreams are an important theme in the play, and many characters have their own dreams and hopes for the future. Choose a character and describe and discuss their dreams – and how this relates to the significance of the title of the play and where it comes from (the poem *Harlem 2* from *Montage of a Dream Deferred*).

Model answer (Beneatha):

Being a doctor

Beneatha is one of the characters in the play who has clear ideas about her dreams and her future. She wants to be a doctor (see p. 36), and so she has to study for a long time. She has more education than any of her relatives, which becomes clear whenever she argues with her brother, who is generally sullen and brutish, or her mother, who won't tolerate Beneatha's educated blasphemy (see pp. 50–51). Ironically, Walter, who complains so much about other people not supporting him enough when it comes to his dreams, is arrogantly dismissive of Beneatha's desire to study and become a doctor: "[...] just get married and be quiet", he tells her (p. 38).

Modern woman

But Beneatha doesn't believe that her dreams and her future have to be defined by being a wife to a man who will run her life.

When her mother and Ruth confront her about her relationship with George Murchison, she says that she is going to be a doctor, and only then will she think about getting married – "if I ever get married" (p. 50). She is a strong and independent-minded young woman, and modern in the way she seeks to pursue her own dreams rather than conforming to traditional, socially prescribed patterns. Her dream of becoming a doctor comes from an incident in her childhood (pp. 132–133) – "I wanted to cure." (p. 133).

Express herself

Beyond this practical dream she has for her future, Beneatha pursues other dreams which are related to her desire to express herself (see pp. 47–48). She is currently learning guitar; she has learned photography, taken riding lessons, and been in a drama club.

Beneatha also dreams of Africa and her African heritage: Inspired by Joseph Asagai and the gifts he brings her (Nigerian clothes and records), she play-acts at being African (rather than African-American – see pp. 76–79). This dream is a fantasy. Less concrete than her plans to become a doctor, and related to her desire to express herself with her various attempts to learn instruments or other artistic skills, the fantasy of Africa she shares in this scene with Walter is a strange mixture of child-like pantomime and trance-like vision of a mythical shared origin in a place and a culture neither of them has ever seen.

Destroyed dreams

The negative meaning of the title and where it comes from (Langston Hughes' poem *Harlem 2*, about what happens to dreams when they are inhibited) apply to Beneatha most clearly in Act III (pp.132–133). After having learned that Walter has lost all the family's money, she realises that she will no longer be able to study (college education is very expensive in the USA). Being confronted with this brutal reality, she is, in a way, inside the poem. Her dreams have been deferred. The young woman who was so positive, energetic, and confident in her ability to make her dreams real is now crushed by the same bitterness afflicting her brother. She attacks Asagai for his optimism: "You with all your talk and dreams about Africa! You still think you can patch up the world." (p. 133) Her vision of the world is now of a place run by "crooks and thieves and just plain idiots" (p. 133). Most negatively, she says later: "Well – we are dead now. All the talk about dreams and sunlight that goes on in this house. It's all dead now." (p. 143)

But by the end of the play, when she has seen her brother face down Karl Lindner and re-assert himself, her mood has swung back, and she can once again see her dreams clearly: "To go to Africa, Mama – be a doctor in Africa..." (p. 150)

Task 2 **

George calls Walter "Prometheus". Find out who Prometheus was (he is a figure from Greek mythology) – what do you think about George's use of the name here? Is he right – is there something Promethean about Walter? Think about what we know of George's status and character when answering this question.

Model answer:

Greek mythology

Prometheus is a son of the Titans in Greek mythology. He is most famous for having stolen fire from the gods to give to mankind. For this crime, he was chained to a rock for the rest of time, and every day an eagle, the symbol of Zeus, leader of the gods, would tear open his body and eat his liver. Every night his liver would grow back, and so his torment was eternal.

Prometheus is a rebel who challenges authority. As his story is remembered, he saves the human race from the gods and the consequences of their actions, and steals the sacred fire from Olympus to help mankind. George Murchison calls Walter Lee "Prometheus" (p. 86), which Walter doesn't understand. Is it meant as an insult?

If we compare Walter with Prometheus, we can say that Zeus and the gods of Olympus represent the authorities and are symbols of oppression and repression. For Walter the equivalent forces are the structural economic and racial injustices of the system in which he lives. Zeus and the gods can be roughly equated with "the establishment" – the white power structure.

The equivalent to the fire in Prometheus' story would then probably be the money, it would seem, but George Murchison doesn't know about this (or at least, we have no indication that he knows anything about it). So what is it he thinks Walter/Prometheus is stealing?

George tells Walter he is "all wacked up with bitterness" (p. 85), to which Walter replies: "Don't you see no stars gleaming that you can't reach out and grab? [...] Here I am a giant – surrounded by ants!"

Rebel

This would seem to be the key to what George means when he calls Walter Prometheus. The main point he is making is the idea of rebellion: Prometheus, like the fallen angel Lucifer in Christianity (in particular in John Milton's *Paradise Lost* (1667), is a rebel against powerful, godlike authority. Walter has ambition and feels oppressed and held down by what he perceives as powerful forces – everything from unsupportive black women to anyone who fails to acknowledge how wonderful his ideas are – and his attempt at rebellion involves using his dead father's life insurance money to invest in a liquor store.

George's use of the name Prometheus is only partly relevant. Walter is an angry rebel, but he is not driven to save his fellow man by bringing the gift of fire (warmth, comfort, light) – not by any stretch of the imagination. Nothing we know about Walter suggests that he would use any power or wealth he had to help the people around him. So as far as the idea of Prometheus applies to Walter, we can say that yes, he is a rebel, but no, the significance and symbolism of the Promethean myths do not really apply to Walter Lee Younger.

As for George, it appears that his use of the name is a casual effort to annoy Walter. We know that George comes from a wealthy, middle-class family – a very different and much more privileged background than Walter. He must surely know that Walter is not particularly well-educated and would probably not know who or what Prometheus was. And while George understands, it seems, that Prometheus is a rebel who raged against authority, like Walter, he seems not to know, or at least from the context we can assume that he doesn't understand, what the wider and deeper elements of the Promethean myth are and what they mean. His use of the name is half-right and half-understood.

Task 3 **

The word *assimilationism* is used a few times in the play. It is usually presented as being a bad thing. Find out what the word means and discuss the positive and negative aspects – as it is presented in the play.

Model answer:

Assimilationism is an old word and is no longer really used today. Nowadays, people use the term "cultural assimilation". To assimilate means "to become, or allow somebody to become, a part of a country or community rather than remaining in a separate group"[33].

---

33 Oxford Advanced Learners Dictionary

The -ism suffix attached means that the word to which it has been attached is a conscious and organised ideology or movement or philosophy: assimilationism therefore means (in the context of *A Raisin in the Sun*) a concerted effort to make African-Americans assimilate into mainstream American society at the expense of their African heritage and cultural roots.

The word is used in the play in a mostly negative way. When Asagai suggests to Beneatha that black people in America are assimilated, she responds angrily "I am not an assimilationist!" (p. 62–64). Beneatha wants to feel pride in her African-ness, and she is rejecting the example of George Murchison, who represents the "assimilationist" black American, in favour of the more sophisticated, thoughtful and rooted, Joseph Asagai.

Music

But Beneatha's passionate rejection of "assimilationism" has ironic and almost comic tones. When she launches into her full-scale Nigerian pantomime (pp. 76–81), she turns off the music which had been playing "with an arrogant flourish" (p. 76). The music is described in the stage directions as "*good loud blues*". But Beneatha says: "Enough of this assimilationist junk!" and replaces the blues record with some one of Asagai's Nigerian music.

Her behaviour here is comic and colourful and entertaining, and it looks more like someone playing fancy-dress, or wearing a disguise, or trying out a new look, than something really deep. But this is a more complex matter, because we see both Beneatha and Walter come under a kind of spell when they dance to the music. And Beneatha is not a casual dabbler in African topics: she is educated. She can challenge anyone around her on the subject of the proud accomplishments of the neglected and lost kingdoms of Africa.

Uncle Tom's Cabin

The word is also used at the end of this episode, when George arrives. Beneatha says, "I hate assimilationist Negroes!" (p. 81) and Ruth is confused, not knowing what the word is supposed to mean.

George, flippantly, says "it's just a college girl's way of calling people Uncle Toms". Uncle Tom is the famous character from Harriet Beecher Stowe's 1852 novel *Uncle Tom's Cabin*. Tom is most commonly used as a term of abuse for someone who is too servile or obedient. George is here suggesting that Beneatha uses the word assimilationist to attack non-radical black people – people like George, who adapt and assimilate to mainstream, white-dominated American culture and society – in the same way that other people would call them Uncle Toms.

The way the word is used in the play is interesting. It is both valid and silly: On one hand it is suggested that it is not good for African-Americans to lose connection to their heritage and origins. But Beneatha's wild and enthusiastic embrace of the term, in particular given the pantomime-like context of her in all her borrowed Nigerian finery, has the feel of something being tried on for size, an experiment in exploring identity.

In conclusion, we could say that the word assimilationism itself might be a little silly – or even too aggressive and polemical – but the concept behind it is real and worthy of exploration.

SOURCES & REFERENCES

Edition used for this study guide:

Hansberry, Lorraine: *A Raisin in the Sun*. Stuttgart: Klett Sprachen / Vintage, New York, 2017.

About the author:

Strain, Tracy Heather; Schultz, Chiz; MacLowry, Randall: *Sighted Eyes / Feeling Heart*. 2017. https://www.sightedeyesfeelingheart.com → A documentary feature about Lorraine Hansberry.

Anderson, Michael: *Lorraine Hansberry's Freedom Family*. In: *American Communist History*, Volume 7, Number 2, 2008. https://www.tandfonline.com/doi/abs/10.1080/14743890802580131?journalCode=rach20

Hansberry v. Lee, 311 U.S. 32 (1940). https://supreme.justia.com/cases/federal/us/311/32/

About *A Raisin in the Sun*:

Lorraine Hansberry Interview (1959). https://www.youtube.com/watch?v=ZkFR_6DGJ3o → Hansberry discusses *A Raisin in the Sun*.

Lorraine Hansberry's Inspiration for "A Raisin in the Sun". (2018). https://www.youtube.com/watch?v=z9IFbBCFa0Y

Bernstein, Robin M.: *Inventing a Fishbowl: White Supremacy and the Critical Reception of Lorraine Hansberry's A Raisin in the Sun*. 1999. In: *Modern Drama* 42(1): 16–27. https://dash.harvard.edu/handle/1/3659695 → An essay about racist reactions to the play.

Brennan, Claire: *A Raisin in the Sun review – still challenging its characters and audience*. In: *The Guardian*, 7.2.2016.

https://www.theguardian.com/stage/2016/feb/07/a-raisin-in-the-sun-review-lorraine-hansberry-crucible → Review of a 2016 production.

Bruckner, D. J. R.: *At Roundabout, 'A Raisin in the Sun'*. In: *New York Times*, 15.8.1986. https://www.nytimes.com/1986/08/15/theater/stage-at-roundabout-a-raisin-in-the-sun.html → Review of the 1986 production.

Gillespie, Blake: *Macklemore Is Getting Major Flack On Twitter For This Literary Fail*. In: *MTV news*, 8.5.2015. http://www.mtv.com/news/2233606/macklemore-a-raisin-in-the-sun-fail/

Rich, Frank: *Raisin in the Sun Anniversary in Chicago*. In: *New York Times*, 5.10.1983. https://www.nytimes.com/1983/10/05/theater/theater-raisin-in-sun-anniversary-in-chicago.html → Review, emphasising the play's historical importance.

Film *A Raisin in the Sun*:

Raisin in the Sun (German title: *Ein Fleck in der Sonne*) 1961 → The DVD is easily available and not expensive: the film is also available on streaming services.

Pan-Africanism:

http://exhibitions.nypl.org/africanaage/essay-pan-africanism.html → This topic is very interesting in itself, and is highly relevant to any deeper study of Lorraine Hansberry's work and ideas. The link is to a good web hub with links to many other aspects of the topic of Pan-Africanism.

Other references:

Mann, Iris: *'To Be Young, Gifted and Black' Belongs More to the Page Than the Stage*. In: *Backstage*, 11.2.2013.

https://www.backstage.com/magazine/article/young-gifted-black-belongs-page-stage-44840/

Ousby, Ian (ed.): *The Cambridge Guide to Literature in English*. Cambridge: Cambridge University Press, 1988. → An excellent standard reference work for biographical and bibliographical information on English-language literature.

Peck and Baldwin: *I Am Not Your Negro*. London: Penguin Modern Classics, 2017.

Sandburg, Carl: *Chicago*. 1914. https://www.poetryfoundation.org/poetrymagazine/poems/12840/chicago

White, Edmund: *Genet*. London: Chatto & Windus, 1993. → This is the major biography of Jean Genet, author of *The Blacks*, the play which inspired Hansbery to write *Les Blancs*.

Zacher, Scotty: *Clybourne Park* (Steppenwolf Theatre). In: *Chicago Theater Beat*, 21.9.2011. http://chicagotheaterbeat.com/2011/09/21/review-clybourne-park-steppenwolf-theatre/ → Review

(All Internet pages last retrieved on 11.5.2019.)

A note on Wikipedia as a research tool:

As usual, Wikipedia can provide a good starting point for research and information. Summaries of more esoteric subjects which are only marginally relevant – like the court case involving Hansberry's father and the influence it had on the plot of *Raisin* – can be easily researched using Wikipedia.

But it is always important to make the effort to go a few steps beyond and follow links to original sources. Wikipedia is an unstable platform, and inaccuracies and flat-out lies can be all too easily smuggled into its articles. Other sources which have been through more rigorous quality control procedures – like reference works from established publishers, or original sources like newspapers – are infinitely preferable as sources for any kind of academic or serious work.

INDEX